CROSSROADS OF COMMERCE

A History of Free Enterprise in Oklahoma

Dr. Bob Blackburn

Printed in the United States of America
for the Oklahoma Historical Society.
Design by Cynthia Manning.

All images courtesy of the Oklahoma Historical Society (OHS) unless
otherwise noted.

On the Cover: TG&Y all decked out for Easter. (The Beryl Ford Collection/
            Rotary Club of Tulsa, Tulsa City- County Library and
            Tulsa Historical Society)

This book is dedicated to all the entrepreneurs that have contributed to Oklahoma's thriving economy.

CROSSROADS OF COMMERCE:
A History of Free Enterprise in Oklahoma

Author's Preface

When I joined the Oklahoma Historical Society team in 1979 as editor of *The Chronicles of Oklahoma*, I noticed several gaps in the way our predecessors had collected, preserved, and shared the story of our state and its people. Some of the gaps were chronological, such as a shortage of materials on the twentieth century. Other gaps were geographical or thematic, with little collected on subjects such as the Panhandle, African Americans, women, and popular culture.

Surprisingly, one of the most glaring gaps was the history of free enterprise in the twin territories and state. There were a few isolated collections and exhibits, usually in the context of tribal history or biography, but there had never been an attempt to aggressively pursue the connected stories of businessmen and women who took the risks, invested in enterprises, and drove the wheels of economic development. Over the past thirty years we have started to fill that gap.

This book is a peek into the world of free enterprise in Oklahoma as represented in two galleries in the Oklahoma History Center. One of the exhibits is topical because it overshadows everything else since statehood. Of course, that is the story of oil and gas. The other exhibit is chronological, spanning three centuries with stories pulled from agriculture, retail, services, manufacturing, transportation, broadcasting, entertainment, sports, and tribal enterprise. This book, as with the exhibits, is not meant to be a comprehensive story of economic development. Rather, we have used select stories to connect the dots of Oklahoma's evolving economy as the stage of history turned with challenges and opportunities.

Although my name is on the book as the principal curator and author, the stories reflect the work of many individuals who helped with the research, writing, editing, artifact selection, and design process. I want to thank everyone who contributed to the effort. You know who you are. I also want to thank the donors, led by George Records and Marvin Jirous, who contributed more than $1.6 million to make the Crossroads exhibit and book possible. Without our partners, the Oklahoma Historical Society could not sustain the quality and volume of work necessary to fulfill our mission to collect, preserve, and share our history.

Please enjoy this stroll to and through Oklahoma's crossroads of commerce.

Bob L. Blackburn, Ph.D.
Executive Director,
Oklahoma Historical Society

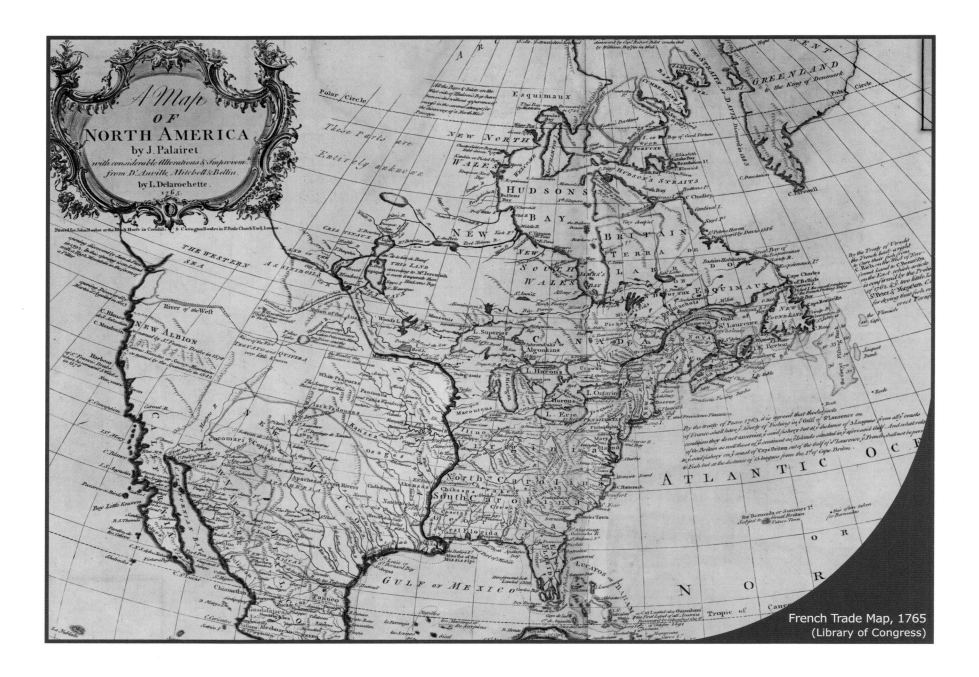

French Trade Map, 1765
(Library of Congress)

Chapter One

Conquering Distance

From 1719 to 1907, American Indians and pioneers found ways to invest in trade and business on a landlocked frontier. At times, the best course was a community working together, such as the Wichitas, Comanches, and Osages who defended their hunting grounds and selected trade partners. At other times, the formula for success was survival of the fittest, one merchant competing against others. From trails and rivers to horses and trains, this changing frontier posed challenges… and opportunities.

One of
a series of
paintings by
George Catlin
illustrating the
exploration of
LaSalle (1678-1687)
(published by Arkansas Heritage
and made by DEXTER PRESS,
West Nyack, New York)

World Markets and Indian Trade

American Indians had three ways to acquire material wealth on the early Oklahoma frontier before 1803. They could produce it. They could take it away from someone else by force. Or they could earn it through trade. The bounty of Oklahoma's natural resources, combined with a growing American Indian demand for guns and other manufactured goods, made Oklahoma a crossroads of world trade from 1719 to 1803.

Indian Warrior
(OHS)

The Wichitas: Middlemen of the Southern Plains

The Caddoan-speaking tribes, including the Wichitas, had deep roots in long distance trade. From the 800s to the 1400s, trade items passing through the Southern Plains included shells from the Gulf Coast, pipestone from the Great Lakes, obsidian and turquoise from the desert Southwest, and feathers from Mexico. In 1719, when the French adventurer Jean-Baptiste Bénard de la Harpe arrived in the future state of Oklahoma, a new chapter in frontier trade opened.

On one side of this trading opportunity were the nine autonomous villages of the Wichitas located along the banks of the Arkansas River above the Three Forks. They often had surplus crops of beans, corn, and squash, as well as herds of horses and stacks of skins and buffalo hides. On the other side were French merchants operating out of New Orleans who had guns, powder, and ammunition, as well as manufactured items such as knives, vermillion, and cloth. Each side wanted what the other had.

Within a few decades, the typical Wichita trading village included several hundred warriors and their families, numerous grass huts, and a fortification of earth and timber surrounded by a deep moat up to nine feet wide. Every spring, the French paddled or poled canoes or flatboats up the Arkansas River to trade with the Wichitas. While the French returned to Arkansas Post, Natchitoches, and New Orleans with their goods, the Wichitas in turn traded with other tribes to the north and west.

In 1747 the French encouraged an alliance between the Wichitas and their traditional enemies, the Comanches, who soon joined the trade network that stretched from France to the Southern Plains. Ten years later, pressed southward by the well-armed Osages, the Wichitas and Comanches moved their primary villages to the Red River, where they were besieged by a Spanish army in 1759. Despite the use of two small cannons, the Spanish forces could not breach the palisades built by the Wichitas and their Comanche allies.

In addition to leaving behind their manufactured goods, the French left a legacy of place names that filled in the maps needed by European merchants. Waterways, used as the lifelines of commerce, thus became the Arkansas, the Verdigris, the Canadian, the Poteau, the Kiamichi, and the River Rouge, better known as the Red River.

Trade with Comanches by Charles Shaw.
(Texas Beyond History and University of Texas)

The Wichita and the French

The Wichitas and their Comanche allies traded with the French who willingly supplied guns, powder, and ammunition. The Spanish, with outposts in Santa Fe and San Antonio to the west and south, refused to trade guns to Indians and insisted that the nomadic tribes become farmers and live adjacent to missions where they could be converted to the Catholic faith.

In the 1700s France enjoyed unprecedented prosperity, but most of the wealth was concentrated at the top of society under the control of the king and a growing aristocracy. The king's Banque Royale (Royal Bank) sold stock in the Compagnie Perpetuelle des Indes (Perpetual Company of the Indies), which in turn underwrote expeditions into Indian country and provided the money to buy guns, powder, ammunition, and trade goods.

French bank note
(National Numismatic Collection at the Smithsonian Institution)

Compulsory conversion of native Americans to christianity by Spanish Jesuit missionaries in the 16th century
(Arizonia Historical Society)

Who were the Kitikiti'sh?

The Wichita people refer to themselves as the Kitikiti'sh or "Raccoon Eyes" in reference to their old practice of facial tattooing. However, the word Kitikiti'sh is probably not Wichita in origin. The first appearance of this word is in the journal of French explorer Jean-Baptiste Bénard de la Harpe recording the first European contact with the Wichitas on the Arkansas River near present-day Tulsa. While the first part of the word does contain the Wichita root word for eyes, it does not contain anything resembling the word for raccoon. Also, the structure of the word is seemingly reversed. In the Wichita language, Kitikiti'sh would be the combination of raccoon plus eyes. Instead, Kitikiti'sh seems to be derived from eyes plus an unknown word.

Contemporary elders theorize that perhaps the word could be a name used by La Harpe's Caddo translators, a misheard pronunciation, or a part of a truncated sentence lost during translation from Wichita to Caddo to French.

by Matt Reed

Painting of a Wichita Woman
(Gilcrease Institute)

Wichita man
(Smithsonian Institute)

Osage Trade and the Chouteau Dynasty

At the end of the French and Indian War, the Osages dominated a rich swath of land from the Ozark Plateau south and west into what is now Missouri, Kansas, Oklahoma, and Arkansas. To improve trade relations with the Osages, two French-speaking merchants born in New Orleans established the village of St. Louis in 1764. The founders were the half- brothers Auguste and Pierre Chouteau.

While Auguste built a fortune from trade, real estate, and banking, Pierre was a frontiersman who lived among the Osages, learned their language, and earned their trust. In 1796, with the Wichitas and their Comanche allies confined to palisaded forts on the Red River, several thousand Osages migrated to the rich fur-bearing lands along the Arkansas, Verdigris, and Grand Rivers. Pierre, with a monopoly on Osage trade, established a year-round trading post on the Grand River at what is now the town of Salina. Within two years, the Chouteau family controlled more than half of all trade goods moving through St. Louis.

Pierre's son, later referred to as Colonel A. P. Chouteau, expanded the Osage trade even more. He constructed a trading post on the Verdigris River and imported approximately $20,000 worth of trade goods each year. In return, the Osages brought in tanned deer hides, beaver pelts, and furs from bear, raccoon, and otter, all wrapped in buffalo hides. A. P.'s brother, Pierre Jr., often referred to as Cadet, expanded the trade network up the Missouri and Mississippi Rivers.

Pierre Choteau's great-great-great granddaughter, Yvonne Chouteau, would gain fame not as a trader but as a dancer. In 1943, at the age of 14, she joined the Ballet Russe de Monte Carlo and earned a place as one of Oklahoma's celebrated five Indian ballerinas.

Jean Pierre Chouteau (1758-1849), American fur trader and pioneer, by Charles Henry Granger (OHS)

Mill with Waterwheel attributed to Henry Harris, dated before 1874. (Royal Birmingham Society of Artists)

Turning the Wheels of Commerce

As the people of the Five Civilized Tribes rebuilt their lives and homes in Indian Territory, they needed local industry to convert crops and raw materials into consumer products that could be used or sold. They also needed an efficient mode of transportation to export their products and import manufactured goods. One resource that served both needs was water.

River Boat
(Louisiana State University)

Investing on Flint Creek: Hildebrand-Beck's Mill

One Cherokee businessman who used water to turn the wheels of commerce was Stephen Hildebrand. His father was a native-born German and his mother was a Cherokee citizen. Stephen grew up among his Cherokee kinsmen in Tennessee, where his father and uncles operated saw and grist mills. He brought his Cherokee citizenship and milling experience to Indian Territory after the Trail of Tears and married Polly Beck, a Cherokee whose uncle had built a water-powered grist mill on Flint Creek in 1845.

By the 1850s Cherokee farmers were producing bumper crops along Flint Creek, where thick stands of timber grew on the rocky slopes of the valley. The Hildebrands decided to invest in the mill. They paid two Irishmen $2,000 in gold to expand the three-quarters-mile-long water chase from four feet by four feet to eight

Beck's Mill
(OHS)

feet by eight feet through solid rock. Then they added a saw mill operation, which became the real profit center of the enterprise.

The mill originally ground corn and wheat. Two sets of marble buhr millstones, both imported from France, were powered by an over-shot water wheel that was 20 feet in diameter. On a good day, the mill could grind from 12 to 20 bushels of grain per hour. As stipulated in the Laws of the Cherokee Nation, the grist mill owner kept one-eighth of the processed grain as a fee. The saw mill generated even more profits as Cherokees and non-Indian families built homes, barns, and stores after the Civil War. From the 1870s to the 1960s, the mill was operated by Beck family members related to Polly Beck Hildebrand.

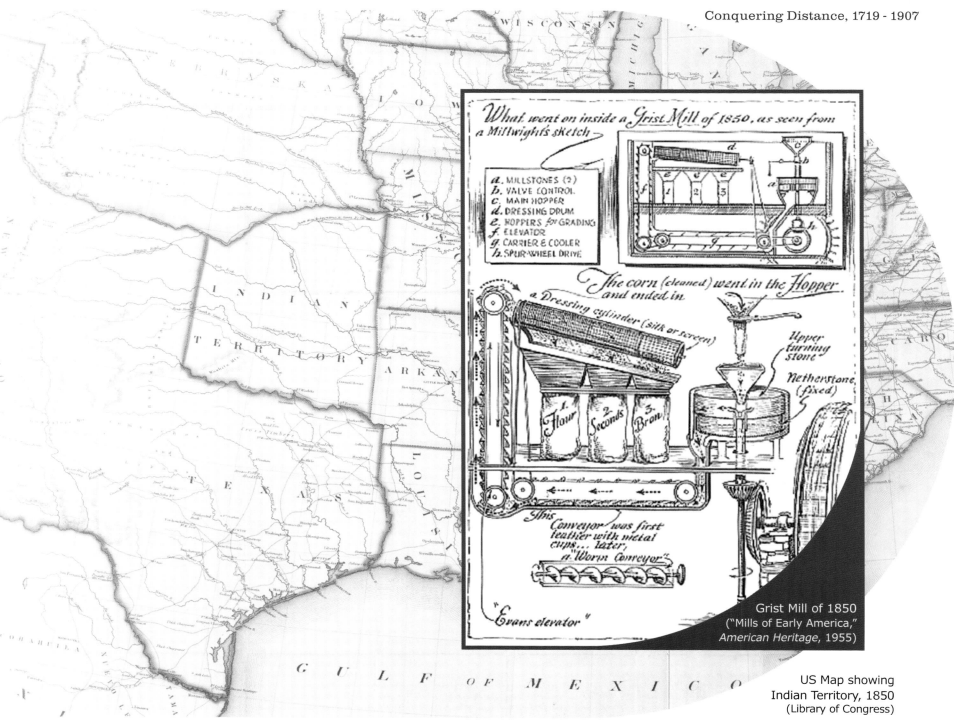

Grist Mill of 1850
("Mills of Early America,"
American Heritage, 1955)

US Map showing
Indian Territory, 1850
(Library of Congress)

The Richest Man West of Natchez

The most efficient way to ship goods and people over long distances in frontier Oklahoma was by river. One man who built an economic empire along these arteries of trade was Choctaw entrepreneur Robert M. Jones.

Jones was raised with one foot in the world of his Choctaw mother and one foot in the world of his white father. After attending the Choctaw Academy in Kentucky, he was hired to drive a herd of horses from Mississippi to Indian Territory during the Choctaw Trail of Tears. Jones settled near Fort Towson, close to the Red River, and married Susan Colbert, the daughter of a successful planter.

In 1836, the same year he married into the Colbert clan, Jones opened his first trading post in a little community called Doaksville. Two years later the Red River was cleared for riverboat traffic, which gave Jones an efficient way to import manufactured goods and export crops and raw materials that could be sold in New Orleans. He imported the first cotton gin to Indian Territory, expanded to 28 stores, owned two river boats, and operated six plantations, one with more than 5,000 acres planted to cotton.

Jones served the Choctaw people while building his businesses. During the Civil War he was a delegate to the Confederate Congress in Richmond, Virginia. After the war he was a member of the Choctaw delegation that negotiated the Reconstruction Treaty of 1866.

Robert M. Jones (OHS)

Home of Robert M. Jones, Rose Hill (OHS)

Salt of the Earth

Water also served as a source for salt. As a food preservative, salt conquered time. As an additive to preserve hides for market, it conquered distance. Cherokee merchant John Rogers found a way to tap groundwater for a steady supply of salt to meet this growing demand.

Rogers was principal chief of the Western Cherokees in 1830 when he purchased the salt works that Pierre Chouteau had established near present-day Salina. Rogers bought the improvements from Sam Houston, his brother-in-law, who soon would become famous as the first president of Texas. Rogers expanded the salt works and invested in the little self-sufficient community. He dug new wells, purchased 115 large kettles, cultivated 25 acres of crops, planted 40 acres of fruit trees, and added numerous cabins. By 1838 his workers were producing an average of 80 bushels of salt a day.

The process of making salt began by pulling water from the saline wells and boiling the water in kettles until only salt was left behind. Slaves moved the commodity to the salt house, where it was dried and loaded onto wagons or into bags and barrels for sale to local settlers. Rogers also exported salt down the Arkansas River by riverboat to New Orleans. Rogers prospered in this trade until 1844 when the Cherokee Nation leased the salt works to Lewis Ross, the brother of Principal Chief John Ross. Cost of the lease was $1,600 a year.

In 1859 Lewis Ross was digging additional saline wells when his workers hit a black, sticky substance. They quickly abandoned that well and dug in another spot. That black, sticky substance, worthless to them, was oil.

Interior view of Salt-Works (*Harpers Weekly*, 1-14-1865)

Jefferson's Salt Mountain

Major George C. Sibley, US Indian Agent, 1856 (OHS)

In 1811 President Thomas Jefferson sent an expedition into what would become Oklahoma to improve relations with the Pawnee, Kansa, and Osage Indians and search for the fabled "salt mountain," which if real, would have great commercial value. The expedition was led by George Champlin Sibley, a 29-year-old frontiersman who would gain fame as a soldier, politician, and educator. Sibley's small party traveled west from Kansas City until they found what is now called the Great Salt Plains in present-day Alfalfa County. He described the salt flats as a "brilliant field of snow," and remarked that "the salt was unquestionably superior to any that I ever saw." Although there was no mountain, the legend of a land covered by salt turned out to be true.

The Commerce of Exploration

In 1853 the US Congress authorized three surveys to find the best route for a railroad to California. Led by Lt. Amiel Weeks Whipple, one of those surveys started from Fort Smith, Arkansas, and followed the California Road west through the central part of the Indian Territory. Along the way the explorers described natural resources with commercial value such as coal, water, and timber. Despite the advantages of what would later become part of the famous Route 66 highway, regional rivalries and the Civil War pushed the first transcontinental railroad farther north to Nebraska. The first railroad into Indian Territory would be delayed until 1871.

Steam train (Public Domain)

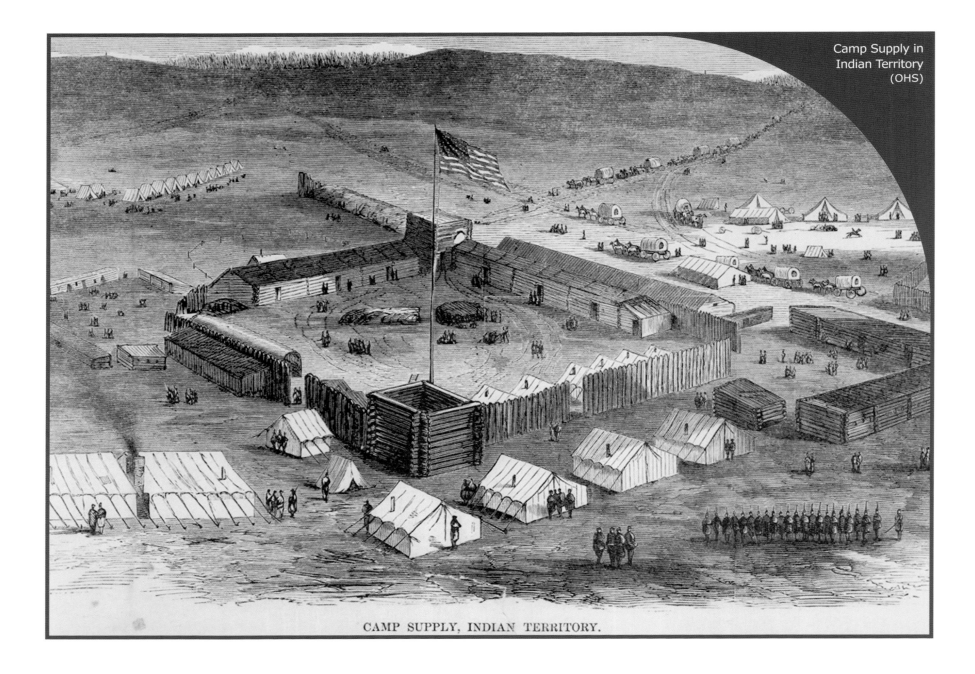

Camp Supply in Indian Territory (OHS)

CAMP SUPPLY, INDIAN TERRITORY.

Frontier Merchants in Indian Country

From 1803 to 1892, more than 40 tribes were removed to or confined to Indian Territory in what is now Oklahoma. As tribal members rebuilt their lives and communities, they needed access to the outside world as a market for their surplus products and as a steady source of manufactured goods for consumption. Frontier merchants helped conquer the limitations of distance as they met both needs.

1889 Map of Indian Territory
(OHS)

Frederick Severs

Frederick Severs was a frontier entrepreneur. Born and raised in Arkansas, he worked in a general store in Fort Gibson and taught in the Creek Nation before the Civil War. He became a friend of Samuel Checote and rose to the rank of captain in the Creek Mounted Volunteers of the Confederate Army. Following the war, he cornered the market on pecans growing in the Arkansas River valley and made enough money to open a store, which he eventually moved to Okmulgee and then Muskogee. Severs diversified into ranching and farming and founded the First National Bank of Muskogee, organized the Muskogee Roller Milling Company, and built the impressive Severs Hotel.

Hotel Severs
(OHS)

J. J. McAlester

J. J. McAlester, a Confederate veteran living in Fort Smith, Arkansas, learned from a friend that vast coal outcrops had been surveyed in the Choctaw Nation near a place called Cross Roads. He moved to the territory, worked at two trading posts, and eventually raised the money to build his own general merchandise store near the coal fields. In 1872 he married Rebecca Burney, the daughter of a future Chickasaw governor, and earned the right to claim land in the Choctaw and Chickasaw Nations.

James J. McAlester, Lt. Govenor of Oklahoma 1910 (OHS)

Sign for J. J. McAlester's store
(OHS)

McAlester used that privilege to claim coal lands adjacent to the newly laid railroad tracks of the Missouri, Kansas, and Texas (KATY) Railroad. He started a mining enterprise, but quickly sold his improvements to a company with the resources for deep shaft mines. The influx of coal miners from England, Italy, Poland, and Russia created new customers. The little community that grew up around his store was named McAlester.

Frederick G. Drummond

Frederick G. Drummond was a Scotsman born in 1864. He immigrated to America at the age of 18 and bounced around the frontier until he landed in St. Louis, where he found a job with a wholesale dry goods company. He soon was hired by one of the firm's customers to work at a trading post in the Osage Nation. In 1886, at the age of 22, Drummond moved to Pawhuska.

Frederick Drummond
(OHS)

While Drummond was learning the Osage language and earning the trust of his customers, he married a young girl from Kansas who saved enough money selling eggs and produce for them to buy a partnership in the Hominy Trading Company in 1903. The timing was perfect. Knowing that oil already had been discovered on their reservation, the Osages demanded that the tribe retain mineral rights in common even though they had to allot surface ownership to individual tribal members. The wealth from that underground reservation flowed through headrights to Osage families and then to stores such as the Hominy Trading Company.

Hominy Trading Post, 1910
(OHS)

Cherokee Telephone Company

Oklahoma's first commercial telephone system was the Cherokee Telephone Company in Tahlequah, Cherokee Nation, founded in 1885 by Ed K. Hicks, a young Cherokee businessman. To convince members of the Cherokee Council to approve his permit, Hicks acquired three telephones in St. Louis and set up a demonstration for them. "Brothers," he said over the line, "this thing can talk Cherokee. It is a good thing." Soon, Hicks and two workers were stringing wire from Tahlequah to Fort Gibson.

Ed Hicks
(OHS)

Love Hotel

Robert Jeremiah Love, a Chickasaw cowboy turned banker and town developer, built the Love Hotel along the Santa Fe Tracks in Purcell in 1895. The brick building was three stories tall with 63 rooms, electric lights, steam heat, a dining room, salesman room, and barber shop. The Love Hotel is now a museum in downtown Purcell.

Love Hotel
ledger of guests
(OHS)

Sod house in Taloga
(OHS)

Claiming the Promised Land

From 1889 to 1907, free land, boom towns, and railroads created new opportunities for business ventures in Oklahoma Territory. At the same time, challenges were sometimes daunting with lax banking laws, scarcity of currency, and uncertainties in a land of immigrants dependent on the success of farmers and ranchers.

Oklahoma City
tent town, week three
(OHS)

Black Ink and Boom Towns

One enterprise born on the first day of the first land run was the State Capital Publishing Company, founded by a daring young man named Frank Greer.

Greer had the skills and temperament for a new frontier. His father was a former soldier and political leader who had served as superintendent of the Kansas Public School System. His brother was a newspaper publisher in Winfield, Kansas. With writing ability, experience in the print shop, and political ambition, young Greer joined a friend and snuck into the Unassigned Lands a day early. At high noon on April 22, 1889, Greer jumped from his hiding place and staked a claim to a town lot in Guthrie.

Greer had with him a stack of *State Capital* newspapers he had printed in Winfield. Thereafter, he would claim he had the first newspaper published in the new territory. Three days after

State Capitol Publishing Company linotype
(OHS)

the land run he sold his lot for $150 and bought a few cases of moveable type and an old job-press. He paid $100 down and took two $100 notes due in 30 and 60 days. Within an hour, the State Capital Publishing Company was doing business on Oklahoma Avenue.

In addition to a daily newspaper, Greer prospered as a job printer. "Everyone was trying to get his sign up and his business started," he later remembered, "so fancy prices were not objected to." For letterhead stationery, he charged $15 per thousand. Envelopes were $12 per thousand. Business cards were $10 per thousand. Greer later added equipment to print and bind law books, ledgers, and Supreme Court reports.

In 1902 Frank Greer built a three-story brick building worthy of his thriving printing business. The State Capital Publishing Building, with its distinctive corner entry topped by a turret, quickly became a landmark. Today, it is a symbol of historic preservation in Oklahoma.

State Capitol Publishing Company bindery
(OHS)

Priming the Pump

On the cash-starved frontier of Oklahoma Territory, the lifeblood of commerce was provided by local bankers who earned the trust of local people willing to deposit their savings with them. In return, bankers loaned the community's pooled money to local people, usually in small amounts backed by collateral.

Perry, Oklahoma, 1894
(OHS)

Fred G. Moore, a Kansan who had attended the US Naval Academy and Princeton, provided this essential service in Perry, Oklahoma Territory, when he chartered the Exchange Bank in 1896. The initial capitalization was $5,000 and the first day's deposits were $1,000. Most loans were for real estate or livestock, which drove the wheels of the economy through the production of cotton, corn, wheat, and cattle. In 1909 Moore hired an assistant cashier named O. R. Hall, who had been born in the Cherokee Outlet before the land run of 1893.

Hall was cashier of the bank in 1933 when the federal government closed every national bank across the country as the Great Depression brought the economy to a grinding halt. The only bank in Noble County to emerge from the bank holiday without recapitalization or reorganization was the Exchange Bank of Perry. Hall, who had become half owner of the bank, was elevated to president and chairman of the board in 1941.

Since that time, the Exchange Bank and Trust Company of Perry has defined family banking. O. R. Hall's son, George, joined the bank in 1950 and served as president and chairman of the board. His son, Charles, came to the bank in 1988 and rose to become chairman of the board. His brother, Zack, was president of the bank in 2015. Today, the Exchange Bank has two branches, one in Perry and one in Stillwater, still earning the trust of local people.

Federal Postal Service

To communicate with the outside world and validate the potential of any rural community, merchants always sought designation for a post office. One unique community that needed that status in 1902 was the All-Black Town of Clearview, founded by John Grayson, Lemuel Jackson, and James Roper at a strategic spot on the Fort Smith & Western Railroad. Grayson, a Creek freedman and son of a former slave, operated the general store where the post office was located, but also dealt in real estate, served as president of the Abe Lincoln Trading Company, and cofounded the local newspaper. The little community prospered until the 1920s as a trade center for Creek freedmen and other African American settlers on surrounding farms.

Clearview Post Office sign
(OHS)

The BIT

   The Bakery of Indian Territory (BIT) was one of the first businesses created in Oklahoma City after the land run of April 22, 1889. It was owned by George Ross after he claimed a lot on West California Avenue. His family, which grew to eight children, lived in the back of the bakery. One of George's grandsons, Bill Ross, later graduated from Classen High School and earned a law degree at the University of Oklahoma. In February 1960, Bill joined a law firm whose principal partner was Streeter Flynn, the son of Oklahoma Territory's first US Senator, Dennis Flynn, and legal counsel for E. K. Gaylord. In 1968 Gaylord asked Bill Ross to represent his daughter, Edith Kinney Gaylord, who with help from Ross created two foundations, the Insasmuch and Excellence and Ethics in Journalism, both of which have already left a legacy of service to the community.

Bakery of Indian Territory, owned by George Ross and located at 6 West Califoria Avenue in Oklahoma City. This photo shows California Avenue looking west from Santa Fe Depot, 1889.
(OHS)

Oldest Family Funeral Home

The Ragsdale Funeral Center, founded in Muskogee in 1896, is still operated by the same family. The founders were William and Malinda Ragsdale, African Americans who moved to Muskogee in 1889 to manage the Creek Indian Livery Barn. They bought the barn seven years later, changed the name to William Ragsdale & Sons Undertaking, and started serving the large African American community that consisted of freedmen living on their allotments, migrants from the Old South, and residents in the All-Black Towns. William and Malinda passed the business to their son, Ted, who in turn passed it to his son, Ted Jr. The family built a new building in 1981.

Ragsdale's Undertaking Company, Indian Territory, Muskogee, 1889
(Anderson-Ragsdale Mortuary)

Twin Territories

Ora Eddleman, a Cherokee woman, became the editor of *Twin Territories: The Indian Magazine* when she was only 18 years old. Her career in journalism started when her family bought the *Muskogee Morning Times*, giving her the opportunity to be a telegraph operator, city editor, and proofreader while still attending school. In 1898 her sister and brother-in-law, Myrta and Walter Sams, asked her to be the editor of a new magazine that would feature stories by American

Indians about American Indians, including news of local interest, club news, works of fiction, and commentary. For the next six years, Ora promoted the preservation of Indian culture, attacked popular stereotypes about Indians, and opened doors of opportunity for Indian authors such as Creek poet Alexander Posey.

Ora Eddleman, 1903
(OHS)

23

Nellie Johnstone Well #1, April 15, 1897 (OHS)

Wooden derricks in Bartlesville, Indian Territory, c. 1900 (OHS)

Chapter Two

Power to Grow

Most Oklahomans take for granted they can put gasoline in their car or turn the knob on a stove and get a blue flame. Similarly, many people give little thought to the fact they drive on good roads, enjoy a growing economy, and reap the benefits of a generous philanthropic community. All of that, either directly or indirectly, can be traced to the history of oil and gas in Oklahoma.

Oklahoma would be a far different state without the vast reservoirs of oil and gas under our feet and the people who search for it, drill for it, produce it, refine it, deliver it, and sell it. Through each step of that process, they give Oklahoma the power to grow.

Gerald M.
Young oil
exploration
(OHS)

New Frontiers in the Search for Oil and Gas

Success in the oil and gas industry has always required two basic building blocks. One is the willingness to take a chance in a high-risk, high-cost business. The other is the technology to get oil and gas out of the ground at a cost below what it sells for in the market place. Oklahomans have been leaders on both fronts.

One early historian called the first generation of oil and gas pioneers the "greatest gamblers." Prominent among them were Oklahomans such as Frank and Waite Phillips, E. W. Marland, H. H. Champlin, William Skelly, and Tom Slick. After World War II, the willingness to take a risk was inherited by another generation of Oklahoma pioneers including Robert S. Kerr, John Kirkpatrick, John and Larry Nichols, Robert Hefner III, George Kaiser, Boone Pickens, Aubrey McClendon, and Harold Hamm.

Postcard showing changing a bit on a cable tool rig post card, c. 1910-1918 (OHS)

Advances in Technology

For the earlier generation, the chance to stay in the business depended on innovations such as seismic mapping, rotary drilling, and down-hole cementing. Each of these technological advances, made during the 1920s with the help of Oklahomans such as John C. Karcher and Erle P. Halliburton, further reduced risk, increased the speed of drilling, and recovered more oil and gas from each well.

After World War II, when most major oil fields in Oklahoma had been discovered and imported oil kept prices for petroleum products at historic lows, success in the oil patch was even more critically linked to advances in technology. Faced with declining domestic drilling in the 1950s, Oklahoma City-based Kerr-McGee pioneered offshore drilling rigs to tap underwater oil fields in the Gulf of Mexico and the North Atlantic. Tulsa-based Helmerich & Payne developed "flex rigs" that could drill faster, use less energy, and move from site to site in less time.

Another strategy was to use new technology to recover oil left behind after the first wave of production. In Osage County, the Burbank Field was discovered in 1920 and produced as much as 85,000 barrels of oil a day. With the limited technology of that time, 80 percent of the oil was still trapped in formations as production declined. In the 1950s Phillips Petroleum pumped water into the field and boosted production from 4,000 to 20,000 barrels of oil per day. Sixty years later, Oklahoma-based Chapparal Energy Corporation returned to the Burbank Field with even newer technology to pump a combination of carbon dioxide and water into the formation. Engineers predict an additional 77 million barrels of oil will be produced from the field over the next 30 years.

Prior to the 1990s, virtually all wells were drilled vertically, straight up and down, in an attempt to pierce a geological formation where oil and gas might be "trapped" as it migrated out of the source rock. If a trap was 10 feet thick, the perforated casing or open flow hole was limited to 10 feet of exposure to the producing zone. Another limitation was the inability to produce oil or gas from "tight" formations, especially source rocks such as shale.

Erle Halliburton at a drilling rig's floor, Harry Sinclair with back to camera, Empire Field
(OHS)

A new frontier, called a "game changer" by many in the industry, was opened in the 1990s with the incremental development of horizontal drilling and hydraulic fracturing. The ability to guide a drill bit from vertical to horizontal as deep as two or three miles below the surface was possible through advancements in gyroscopic compasses, down-hole motors, and measurement-while-drilling tools. For the first time, drillers not only could pierce a producing zone, but they also could reach it and keep the bore hole in it more than a mile in multiple directions from a drilling rig. Oklahomans had helped make it happen.

Just as important was the ability to produce from known source rocks that had previously been too tight to release oil and gas. This revolution was made possible by advances in high-pressure hydraulic fracturing, which had been used in the oil patch since Duncan-based Halliburton performed the first commercial "frac" job in Stephens County on March 17, 1948. By adding trace chemicals and particulates to water and using a new generation of high pressure pumps on the surface, completion crews could open tiny fissures in the rock and create paths for oil and gas to get to the bore hole.

Oklahomans added other technological innovations in well completion and production. On the surface a wellhead called a "Christmas tree" was placed on the well to manage the flow of oil and gas and to control the upward pressure of the well's natural gas and liquids. The Christmas tree provided an assembly of valves to control and route the production of the well. One of the leading manufacturers of wellheads was Downing Wellhead Equipment, Inc. of Oklahoma City, which was founded by Gene and Jo Downing in 1980.

With new technology and the willingness to take a risk, Oklahomans are opening new frontiers in the search for oil and gas.

Postcard showing "Oilfield Near Burbank, Okla." postmarked April 21, 1922 (OHS)

Innovation and the Red Hawk Spar

In 2004 Devon Energy was experimenting with two new innovative technologies to drill for natural gas. In the Gulf of Mexico, Devon teamed with Kerr-McGee to launch a production platform called Red Hawk, the first of its kind. Red Hawk's new "cell spar" design made it inexpensive to build, allowing the pioneering companies to reach deep-water natural gas fields that were too small to target with more expensive, conventional platforms.

That same year Devon was using old technologies in new ways to unlock billions of cubic feet of natural gas from a stingy, unyielding rock called shale. Devon was the first to combine horizontal drilling with hydraulic fracturing in the Barnett Shale, the North Texas field where the shale energy revolution began.

In the end, Devon found success through both advancements, but the enormous impact of horizontal drilling overshadowed the 560-foot-long Red Hawk production platform. With vast volumes of onshore oil and natural gas available through less expensive shale innovations, there was little demand for the marvels of Red Hawk's cell spar technology.

In 2004 Red Hawk had the potential to usher in a new paradigm for deep-water energy production. Years later, because of the shale revolution, Red Hawk became a footnote, obscured by another innovative idea that originated at the same time and from the same place-Oklahoma.

3600-ton Red Hawk deck in the Gulf of Mexico off the coast of Louisiana
(Allison Marine Contractors, LLC)

Decommissioned in September 2014, the Red Hawk Spar was the deepest floating production unit to be retired in the Gulf of Mexico. (Anadarko)

Technician
in the lab
at Kerr-McGee
(OHS)

Natural Gas: From Waste Product to Fuel of the Future

When Oklahoma's first commercial oil well was completed near Bartlesville in 1898, natural gas was considered a waste product with little or no value. At most oil well sites, natural gas was simply flared or vented into the atmosphere.

In 1905 a natural gas pipeline was built from the oil fields south of Tulsa to Oklahoma City, where Oklahoma Gas & Electric intended to generate electricity and distribute gas to homes and businesses for heating and cooking. Fluctuations in seasonal demand were partially offset in the 1930s by underground storage of natural gas in depleted oil fields. Still, the price of natural gas remained low with minimal demand.

Demand rose after World War II as natural gas became an essential ingredient for producing plastics and fertilizer. Meanwhile, domestic use increased as home owners installed central heating and air conditioning units, hot water tanks, yard lamps, and swimming pool heaters. Concerned that the cost of natural gas was going up with demand, Congress imposed price controls on interstate shipments of natural gas in 1954. The result was an artificially low price and few incentives to drill for new reserves.

Oklahoma Gas & Electric Company, Noble Street power plant and sub station, c. 1913 (OHS)

33

The Deep Gas Boom

While federal regulations discouraged exploration for natural gas in the 1960s and 1970s, the artificially low price stimulated demand and caused shortages in many parts of the country. Congress responded by creating two tiers of natural gas pricing—old gas with price controls and new gas with no limits.

As that political drama was unfolding, Oklahoma pioneers such as Robert Hefner III were proving that vast quantities of natural gas could be tapped at depths exceeding four miles underground. Although expensive to drill, prolific gas wells in the Deep Anadarko Basin of western Oklahoma paid off spectacularly as the price of gas doubled, tripled, and kept rising until it increased more than tenfold. Money to drill flowed into the state and wells were drilled as fast as rigs could be built. One television commercial captured the spirit of the boom: "If you don't have an oil well, get one."

The boom ended as dramatically as it had started. As demand for natural gas dropped after the Recession of 1980 and price controls were lifted, the price of new gas plunged and left a generation of companies overleveraged. On July 3, 1982, the house of cards collapsed with the bankruptcy of Penn Square Bank, followed by the failure of the First National Bank of Oklahoma City three years later. Oklahoma's second great depression had begun.

The demand for natural gas finally rebounded in the late 1990s just as the possibilities of horizontal drilling and hydraulic fracturing opened new frontiers for exploration and production. Driving demand was federal deregulation of power distribution and the construction of a new generation of gas-fired electrical generating plants that reflected the environmental benefits of burning natural gas instead of coal. Oklahoma-based companies such as Chesapeake Energy recognized the trend early and went long on gas, buying proven reserves and grabbing mineral rights when the price hovered around $1 per 1,000 cubic feet. As crews cracked the code on releasing natural gas from chalk and shale beds, the price increased to more than $10 per 1,000 cubic feet by 2007. The boom was back.

Although the price of natural gas did not long remain at that lofty level, the ability to drill for and produce the clean-burning fuel in vast quantities with reduced risk was a proven fact. With natural gas deposits underlying all but two counties of Oklahoma, the one-time waste product was suddenly one of the most important natural resources for the future.

Pipes that feed raw natural gas into the plant
(OHS)

The Grand Energy Transition

With vast proven reserves and less risky ways to explore for and produce natural gas, Oklahomans have taken the lead in promoting its use as the fuel of the future.

Robert Hefner III, a third generation Oklahoma oilman, was a natural gas evangelist in the 1960s and 1970s as his crews unlocked the code to giant gas wells in the Deep Anadarko Basin. He lobbied Congress, gave speeches across the country, and eventually published a book called *GET: The Grand Energy Transition* in which he predicted that plentiful and clean burning natural gas could serve as a bridge between the current reliance on imported oil and the possibilities of alternative power sources in the future.

Boone Pickens, an oilman born in Holdenville, Oklahoma, added his voice to the national debate with the Pickens Plan, which included the simple admonition: "Stop America's addiction to imported OPEC oil." A critical part of his plan was the use of natural gas as a fuel for cars and trucks, a theme that was applied at the grassroots level by Aubrey McClendon, the founder of Chesapeake Energy, who adopted the slogan,

Robert Hefner III (OHS)

Aubrey McClendon (McNeese Studios)

"America's Champion of Natural Gas."

The use of natural gas expanded as a result of those efforts. Oklahoma-based retail fuel merchants such as Love's Travel Stops and On-Cue have added compressed natural gas pumps at stations. The State of Oklahoma has converted its fleet of vehicles to compressed natural gas. With cost savings and environmental advantages, the use of natural gas will continue to grow into the future.

168 Dodge Ram 3/4 ton CNG trucks, purchased by the state for use by Oklahoma Department of Transportation, 2013 (State of Oklahoma Office of Management and Enterprise Services)

The World's Most Famous CNG Chopper

As demand for energy increases in the future, natural gas will supplement the critical flow of oil discovered, produced, and delivered by Oklahoma's oil and gas industry. The Chesapeake chopper, built to run on compressed natural gas, is a symbol of that new opportunity.

Chesapeake sponsored the design and construction of the motorcycle, which was built in 2009 on the national television show, *American Choppers*. It has a 117-cubic inch V-Twin engine, a 6-speed transmission, a "fogger" that feeds gas to the engine, an oversized tank for the compressed natural gas, drill bit-inspired details on the handle bars, and a blue-flame color scheme.

The world's first natural gas-powered chopper on display at the Oklahoma History Center (Jeff Briley)

In 2015 Love's
began dispensing
compressed natural gas
at locations on Interstate 40
(Love's Travel Stops)

Kerr-McGee
refinery
(OHS)

Petroleum Refining

The ability to convert crude oil and raw natural gas to useful products such as gasoline, diesel, propane, and helium requires the application of heat, which is controlled by a device called a burner. Jack Zink, a Tulsan raised in "the Oil Capital of the World," built two companies that specialized in the design and installation of burners.

Kerr-McGee refinery
(OHS)

Kerr-McGee burner showing relative size (OHS)

Cracking the Code of Hydrocarbons

Jack's father, John Steele Zink, was a chemist who left a secure job at Oklahoma Natural Gas Company in 1929 to design and sell his own line of commercial burners. By World War II, John was manufacturing floor furnaces from a plant on South Peoria in Tulsa where young Jack learned the hands-on skills of a craftsman in the foundry, machine shop, and assembly plant.

Jack completed a degree in mechanical engineering at Oklahoma A&M, which expanded his ability to predict and measure outcomes. As a sales engineer after the war, he worked with industrial clients to design burners for specific needs in the oil patch. Variables subject to design included the mixture of fuel and oxygen, combustion chamber geometry, thermal input sizes, heat transfer demands, heat release and turn down, firing position, shape of the flame, and ignition. In 1951, to increase efficiency and safety, Jack designed and constructed the world's first test furnace for burners at the plant on Peoria.

John "Jack" Zink (OHS)

With oil refiners as his primary clients, Jack grew the family-owned business from 20 to 300 workers in the 1950s. Then came even more explosive growth in the 1960s and 1970s as his burners were used for flares to burn waste gasses and incinerators to burn hazardous materials. With offices in England, Germany, Italy, and Mexico, the company had more than 600 workers when it was sold to an international corporation in 1981.

In 1983, to once again design and build burners, Jack started a new family-owned company eventually called Zeeco. Many burners were used in gas plants to separate wet from dry gasses and in refineries to heat the heavy hydrocarbons of crude oil and break them down into simpler, lighter products. Since 2000, under the steady hand of Jack's son, Darton, Zeeco has become an international giant. Darton Zink, like his father and grandfather before him, is still driven by the quest to design a better burner.

View inside a Zink burner
(OHS)

Deep Rock
refinery,
Cushing Field, 1940
(OHS)

Transportation in the Oil and Gas Industry

The ability to transport petroleum from here to there has always been critical to the value of crude oil, natural gas, and refined products. During the oil boom era from 1898 to 1929, the most common carriers to and from well sites were railroads and pipelines for long distances and mules and wagons for short distances. By World War I, Cushing was already starting its climb to being the "Pipeline Capital" of the world.

Stacking caseing at Fulkerson Camp, Cushing Field, c. 1910-1918
(OHS)

Pipeline Network

After World War II, the pipeline network in Oklahoma spread like a spider's web connecting well sites with refineries, gas plants with homes, refineries with terminals, and terminals with service stations. Pipeline companies such as Price in Bartlesville and Williams in Tulsa led the way. Trucks, which had been used by gasoline jobbers such as Harold Groendyke since 1932, grew in importance and hauling capacity after the war as super highways crisscrossed the state. Adding to the options for long distance transport of crude oil and refined products after the war was water. Oklahomans, by getting products from here to there, have found ways to add value to what comes out of the ground.

Several family-owned trucking companies still haul fuel and other petroleum products over Oklahoma highways. Some are local jobbers that carry fuel over short distances, such as Red Rock Distributors, with a history dating to 1937 and a service station operated by Barney Brown, Sr., and his two sons in Oklahoma City. From

Mann
pipeline junction
(OHS)

Historical photo of Groendyke tanker truck
(Groendyke Transports, Inc.)

one bobtail trailer that could carry 308 gallons of gasoline to customers such as LeeWay Freight Lines, the company grew to several trucks with a carrying capacity of 9,500 gallons on each load. Today, the fourth generation is involved in managing the company.

Groendyke Transport, headquartered in Enid, is another family-owned trucking firm that specializes in petroleum products. The company was founded by Harold Groendyke in 1932 to haul gasoline from refineries in Enid to customers in the Oklahoma Panhandle. After World War II, the company expanded to hauling a wide range of liquified hazardous products over longer distances. By 2016, under the management of second-generation CEO John Groendyke, the growing fleet had terminals in thirteen states and hauled products from coast to coast.

More recent additions to the family of petroleum transport companies headquartered in Oklahoma are two wholly owned subsidiaries of Love's Travel Stops & Country Stores. One is Gemini Transport, a truck line created in 2001 to haul gasoline and diesel to company stores and third-party customers across the country. The other is Musket Corporation, a fuel-trading and transport arm of Love's based in Houston that uses a fleet of rail cars to haul crude oil as well as refined products. Both subsidiaries give Love's a price advantage and flexibility in the marketplace.

Diamond
service station,
501 S.W. 29th,
Oklahoma City
(OHS)

Fill 'Er Up: The Evolution of Service Stations

Since World War II, the retail business of selling gasoline and diesel for cars and trucks has evolved along with the rest of the oil and gas industry. Some changes have been based on technology. Others have been shaped by market forces. Technology's impact on service stations started with motorized pumps that replaced gravity-flow hand pumps. Later changes included lock-release devices that allowed attendants to service cars while gasoline was pumped, remote reset capabilities that retained control of pumps between users, and credit card readers at the pump.

Grand Opening of a Deep Rock station, Kerr-McGee's move into major retailing, c. 1955 (OHS)

Full-Service to Self-Service

The biggest change was the sudden transition from full-service to self-service. As late as the 1960s, virtually all service stations in Oklahoma were full-service, which included a person who pumped the gasoline, checked engine oil level and tire pressure, and cleaned the windshield. Full-service stations usually included two work bays, one with a lift for light mechanical work and another for washing cars. Extra income was earned by selling tires, batteries, oil, and windshield wipers.

The Arab Oil Embargo of 1973 changed the retail business model of selling fuel. As the price of gasoline doubled and tripled during the shortage, customers looked for the cheapest

Oil embargo of 1973
(National Archives)

prices, which put pressure on profit margins. To cut labor costs, service stations went to self-service, and to replace profits, service stations added mini convenience stores where customers could purchase milk, bread, and other products. Convenience store operators such as Tulsa-based Quik Trip added self-service gasoline pumps, while service station operators such as Tom Love added mini markets.

One attendant cleans the windsheild as another pumps the gas, c. 1960.
(OHS)

Service Station Architecture

To attract customers, service station owners have long used architectural designs that reflect a combination of functional simplicity and popular styles of that era.

When Kerr-McGee opened its first branded full-service gasoline stations in 1965, corporate executives adopted architectural elements such as brushed aluminum finishes, cantilevered roofs, and strong vertical lines inspired by manned space flight and the race to the moon.

The earliest service stations in the state looked like small homes with just enough floor space for one attendant and a few products such as oil, fan belts, and tires. Oklahoma-based companies such as Marland Oil, Phillips Petroleum, and Cities Service built hundreds of service stations in the 1920s and 1930s that adopted European-inspired cottage and Art Deco styles. After World War II, the International style influenced service station design with clean horizontal lines, less adornment, and shiny finishes.

With the fusion of self-service and mini markets with road food and volume sales in the 1980s, service station architecture evolved into a functional combination of a small convenience store and quick-service restaurant surrounded by gas and diesel pump islands with awnings to protect customers.

Knox service station at Northwest Highway in Oklahoma City, 1964 (OHS)

49

DX Pumps and Full Service

The historic gas pumps on display in the Oklahoma History Center were still being used in 1955 when Charles Kemnitz leased the Sunray DX station in Perry, Oklahoma. Three years later, after purchasing the station, he replaced the pumps but kept them in a storage shed.

Kemnitz's son, Craig, started working at the full-service station when he was in the fifth grade, sweeping the floors for 25 cents an hour. By the time he was in the seventh grade, Craig worked weekends and every day after school from 3:30 to 9:00. He got two days off a month, every other Sunday.

In 1977, after buying the agency from DX, Charles and Craig became jobbers who also owned the tanks, fuel, and accounts receivable and sold to other service stations, farmers, and drilling rig operators. A decade later, they picked up their biggest client, Ditch Witch, which became a steady industrial customer for fuel and lubricants. In 2016 the full service Kemnitz Sinclair was the oldest continually operated service station in Oklahoma.

Charles (left) and Craig Kemnitz in front of the DX station in Perry
(Craig Kemnitz)

Kerr-McGee Service Station

When Robert S. Kerr and Dean McGee founded Kerr-McGee Oil Industries in 1946, there were dozens of branded service station chains and thousands of independently operated stations scattered across the state. Some were homegrown, such as Deep Rock, Knox, Skelly, Sinclair DX, Champlin, Apco, Phillips, and Conoco. Others were affiliated with or operated by national brands, such as Texaco, Mobil, Gulf, and Shell. Trying to diversify beyond contract drilling, exploration, and refining, Kerr-McGee entered the retail market.

At first, Kerr-McGee sold gasoline and oil under the brands of Tulsa-based Deep Rock and Enid-based Knox, two Oklahoma companies acquired in 1955 and 1956, respectively. With additional refining capacity and a growing distribution network, Kerr-McGee opened service stations under the corporate name with a line of products such as Blue Velvet motor oil. Kerr-McGee stations quickly spread outside the region as far west as Arizona.

Kerr-McGee was eventually absorbed by Anadarko Petroleum, but the company's legacy of exploring, drilling, producing, refining, transporting, and selling oil and gas is secure as part of Oklahoma's role in the always changing world of energy.

Kerr-McGee
self-service station
(OHS)

Cattle pasture
(OHS)

Chapter Three

Adding Value

From 1907 to 1929, Oklahoma was one of the fastest growing states in the nation with a booming economy powered by the twin engines of oil and agriculture. Business pioneers added value to what was coming out of the rich soil of the new state. Instead of simply exporting cotton, wheat, and livestock, they invested in gins, mills, and packing plants that expanded markets for farmers and created jobs for others. Their success in turn created wealth that was channeled back into new, competitive businesses.

Working
cattle, 1914
(OHS)

Adding Value to Grass

One of Oklahoma's most abundant natural resources has long been grass. From the rolling plains in the west to the mixed prairies in the east, pioneers discovered they could convert grass into money on the hoof. With a handle on the supply side of free enterprise, all they needed was better access to growing national markets. From 1907 to 1929, while the price for cattle almost tripled, demand was met by investors who saw opportunities to add value to grass.

Working cattle, 1914 (OHS)

Wilson & Company

One entrepreneur stepping onto the stage of history was Thomas E. Wilson, an executive with Morris & Company who opened the first big packing plant in Oklahoma in 1910. Financing, in the form of a subsidy, was provided by Oklahoma City businessmen. As they had hoped, the economic impact was transformative. A competing packing plant was soon built nearby and more than 2,400 jobs were created overnight in a city of 50,000 people.

In 1916 Wilson bought the second plant and renamed it Wilson & Company. The complex consisted of a seven-story beef slaughter house, two seven-story cooling buildings, and a seven-story tank house where bones, horns, hoofs, and sticks were rendered into glue. Other buildings included a power house, an oil house, a lard refinery, an oleo refinery, a fertilizer plant, as well as laundries, hide vaults, stables, machine shops, and offices. Nearby was the Armour packing plant with a similar complex and a vast layout of pens and chutes to hold and move livestock.

Wilson & Company would remain a fixture in the economic life of Oklahoma for decades. In 1963, after Armour closed the adjoining plant, Wilson demolished many of its original buildings and constructed a more modern plant that could better compete with smaller, non-union packers operating closer to big feedlots. It was an uphill battle. First came a leveraged buyout, followed by the end of cattle slaughter in 1979 and the end of hog slaughter in 1981. In 1992, with only 300 people still working at the Oklahoma City plant, Wilson closed and an important chapter in Oklahoma's economic development came to an end.

Packing town OKC
(OHS)

Oklahoma National Stockyards

Thomas Wilson and his company created the Oklahoma National Stockyards to supply a daily source of cattle and hogs for the packing plants and create a place for buyers and sellers to conduct business. The investment included extensive pens and the Livestock Exchange Building.

Initially there were 17 commission companies operating independently of the packers. They represented farmers and ranchers until their hogs and cattle were sold. Typically the cost of yardage fees and commission fees amounted to about one percent of the sales price. Some livestock went to the packing plants, but most went to outside buyers.

By the 1950s the Oklahoma City Stockyards was a major market for 300-pound stocker and 700-pound feeder cattle.

Entrance to "Oklahoma National Stock Yards" on Exchange Ave, OKC (OHS)

The biggest day of sales in the Stockyard's history was a Thursday in 1974 when 21,000 cattle were sold by auction in 23 hours and 30 minutes of continual trading. As envisioned in 1910, the Stockyards and packing plants became a crossroads of commerce that connected supply with demand.

View of Stockyards (OHS)

Packing Plants Jobs

The packing plants created thousands of jobs, some with descriptive titles. After the cattle were run up an outdoor ramp to the seventh floor, the "knocker" stunned the animals. In the "killing bed" a "sticker" severed the carotid artery. The "legger" severed the hind legs at the hooves and forelegs at the knees. A "slider" began the skinning process and a "puller" removed the stomach. A "skinner" pulled the hide from the buttocks and a "yacker" removed more of the hide. Other jobs included the "rump sawyer," the "splitter," the "hide dropper," the "neck man," and the "trimmers."

Cows in a feed lot at the stockyard
(OHS)

Meat-cutting training at Chilocco
(OHS)

Schwab & Co.

Schwab & Co. is the oldest fresh and cured meat supplier in Oklahoma. George Peter Schwab, a native of Germany who landed at Ellis Island in 1890, brought his Old World German sausage recipes to Oklahoma City and opened his first plant in 1912. It has remained a family operation for five generations. A key to its success has been retention of the original recipes and smoking process. In 2007 the family invested $2 million in an expansion that included two 600-foot smokehouses where they could smoke hot dogs for two and one-half hours, turkeys for 10 hours, and hams for 12 hours. Of more than 150 different products, one of the most unusual specialty items has been smoked turkey legs. During the State Fair of Oklahoma in 2007, more than 100,000 turkey legs were sold.

Cattleman's Cafe

Cattleman's Café opened in 1910 as a place where farmers, cowboys, commission men, and packers could get a hearty meal at a fair price. In step with the nonstop pace of business in Packingtown, Cattleman's was open 24 hours a day. In 1945 it was purchased by Hank Frey, a professional gambler who used the café to call a $25,000 bet in a craps game. The roller of the dice, Gene Wade, hit a hard six (double threes) and became the new owner. As a salute to the 24-hour policy, Wade threw a set of front door keys in the North Canadian River. Dick Stubbs, an entrepreneur who had opened a steak house in Stillwater and Applewoods in Oklahoma City, bought Cattleman's in 1990. While improving food quality and service, Stubbs carefully retained historic features such as the original café counter and bar stools, the back-lit mural of cowboys and Hereford cattle, and the iconic longhorn front-door handles.

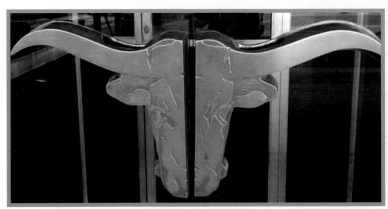

Door handles at Cattleman's
(Nicole Willoughby)

Kamp's Grocery

Henry Herman Kamp was a German immigrant who arrived in Oklahoma City on April 22, 1910. He opened Kamp's Grocery Store and employed a succession of family members. His brother William became the butcher and son Alfred became the baker. As chain grocery stores ramped up competition, the Kamp family responded with higher quality products such as premium meats and baked goods. Although the grocery store at 25th and Classen Boulevard closed in 1996, family members did not give up. Rick Kamp became a chef and worked with John Bennett at the Cellar. Randy Kamp, after becoming an attorney, opened a Johnny Carino's Country Italian Restaurant and Kamp's 1910. Another grandson opened Bill Kamp's Meat Market on North Western. The legacy of Kamp's is still driving the wheels of commerce.

Grinding meat at Kamp's
(OHS)

Man in
cotton field
(OHS)

When Cotton was King

While oil built cities, cotton built communities. Oklahoma's Golden Age of Agriculture started with farmers who planted, chopped, and picked cotton, but the impact of the southern crop cast a wide economic net that included gins, oil mills, compresses, feed producers, buyers, weavers, and clothes makers. From 1907 to 1929, the economy of Main Street Oklahoma depended on the cash generated by King Cotton.

Cotton field
near Waurika
(OHS)

The Rise of King Cotton

Oklahoma became a state just as cotton was becoming king of the cash crops. In 1899, when the price of cotton at the gin was three cents per pound, a farmer could make $25 to $50 per acre with cotton, but only $10 to $15 per acre with wheat and $6 to $13 per acre with corn. By 1907, when the price of cotton rose to 11 cents per pound, the gap in net revenue grew even wider. By statehood, Oklahoma farmers harvested 2,196,000 acres of cotton worth $47,313,727 in fiber, $6,658,303 in seed, and $3,413,896 in oil.

R. K. Wootten, a frontier merchant from Mississippi, saw an opportunity to invest just as cotton's value was rising. In 1899 he purchased the Chickasha Cotton Oil Company in the western part of the Chickasaw Nation in what is now Grady County. On the front end, Wootten reached out to farmers by building gins at country crossroads. Once he bought the cotton, he separated the fiber from the seeds, sold the fiber to buyers usually based out of Galveston, Texas, and shipped the seeds to his oil press where his workers produced edible oil for household use and meal for livestock feed. By 1929 Wootten operated 200 gins and 18 oil mills. His payroll included more than 2,000 workers.

Harrison Gin & Milling Company
(OHS)

Money in the Pocket, Food on the Table

From 1907 to 1929, cotton created hope for a generation of farmers struggling to maintain dignity and preserve a way of life. The threshold for investment was low. Even if they did not own land, they could rent or sharecrop, and with only a mule, a plow, a loan to buy seed, and a bunch of kids to chop and pick, they were in business. If they worked hard, if prices stayed high, if the rains came at the right time, if the boll weevil did not destroy their crop in the field, they had a chance to get ahead.

One farmer who bet his family's future on cotton was Jess Turley, who had been struggling as a sharecropper in the pine woods of southwestern Arkansas. In the fall of 1925, his brother-in-law Tommy Kennedy came to Jess and told him about an opportunity in Oklahoma. He had rented a 160-acre farm in Grady County and planted it fence to fence in cotton. The rains had come, the boll weevils had stayed away, and the crop was ready to pick. He wanted Jess to bring his family out to take shares.

Jess sold a piece of land and bought a Model-T pickup to make the three-day trip west with his wife, Effie, and their seven children, Agnes, John Hill, Travis, Mary, Edgar, Zane, and Lorida. Their eighth child, Ida, was not yet born. Jess spent the next several weeks hauling cotton to the gin and waiting in line to unload. Every time he got back to the farm, the pickers dumped their sacks in the bed and he was off again. By December they had picked almost 100 bales, each weighing 500 pounds, and sold it for 25 cents per pound. After taking out the cost of renting the land, buying the seed, plowing, chopping, and ginning, the net return on that one crop was almost $10,000. Calculating inflation, that was the equivalent of $135,000 in 2015 dollars. For the Turleys and Kennedys, it was money in the pocket, food on the table.

Turley and Kennedy family photo, c. 1925
(OHS)

63

Converting Cotton to Cash

For more than 100 years Round House Overalls has been converting cotton to cash. In 1903 Alvin Nuckolls established the enterprise near the Rock Island Railroad yards and roundhouse in Shawnee, where thousands of workers needed affordable but durable overalls. In 1964, just as denim was becoming a fashion statement for teenaged Baby Boomers, machine shop owner Edward Antosh bought the Round House plant. A decade later his son Jim joined the company and rose to become president in 1986. Since then, Round House Overalls have been sold through retailers such as JC Penny, Walmart, and Atwoods and under brands such as Dickie's and Sherwin Williams. Due in part to the fact that Oklahoma and Texas cotton is used exclusively in the plant, Round House Overalls has gained a cult following in Japan.

Another entrepreneur converting cotton to cash was Minnie Jackson, who came to Guthrie with her family

Round House interior, c. 1900
(Round House)

in 1912. After her husband died in 1922, she adapted her domestic sewing skills and natural salesmanship to producing garments under the brand of Kitty Carol Lingerie. She soon employed more than 40 seamstresses doing piece work in their own homes. Minnie designed the garments, personally trained the workers, and was the chief sales person on the road and in a small shop in Guthrie. Kitty Carol Lingerie, sold in departments stores across the country, earned a reputation as a favorite brand worn by socialites and stage stars.

"They Were Fashioned To Please You"

The little lady who revels in the airy-fairy pastels will be delighted with the vanity sets that we are showing—a step-in, a confiner and a pair of garters to match. They are trimmed with French ponies and come in all colors.

The exotic woman of outre taste will find the thing that is different in the ombre chiffons—vivid, yet very, very lovely under the smart, simple frocks that characterize the mode of today.

Kitty Carol Lingerie
"SPECIAL SPRING EXHIBIT"
105 North Harvey

Kitty Carol advertisement in the *Daily Oklahoman*, 1925
(OHS)

Cotton on the 101 Ranch

In 1926, with cotton selling for more than 25 cents per pound, 101 Ranch pioneer George Miller hired 200 African American farmers and planted 2,000 acres to cotton in the western part of Osage County. To prove that cotton would grow that far north, Miller developed an early maturing variety called Early Bird that could be planted as early as mid-June.

African American workers taking a break on the 101 Ranch (OHS)

Great Depression and King Cotton

From 1925 to 1939, the land planted to cotton in Oklahoma plunged from 5,396,000 to 1,500,000 acres. The reason was simple supply and demand. The Great Depression, coupled with cheap imported cotton, drove the price of cotton down to 5 cents a pound in 1939. After World War II and innovations such as mechanical pickers and irrigation, native cotton production shifted south to the Red River Valley in southwestern Oklahoma.

Weighing full sacks of cotton, November 1949 (National Archives)

Yukon Mills
(OHS)

Farm to Market

As farm families moved onto the Great Plains of central and western Oklahoma in the late 1890s and early 1900s, they found good soil but not enough average rainfall for cotton or corn. Instead, it was perfect for hard winter wheat, which could be planted in the fall and harvested in the late spring and early summer. The challenge was getting it to market or storing it until the crop was either sold or milled into flour. Onto this stage of history stepped investors who built commercial grain elevators.

Postcard showing
"Wheat Harvest in Oklahoma," 1907
(OHS)

Country Elevators

Dobry Mill
(OHS)

Most country elevators were owned by individual investors such as Frank and William Wheeler, natives of Indiana who opened Wheeler Brothers Grain Company in Watonga in 1917 with a small wooden elevator built next to the railroad tracks. William's son, Gene, expanded the company with its first concrete elevator in 1945, followed by investments in feed lots and a dry bulk fertilizer blending plant. At the dawn of the 21st century, Wheeler Brothers owned a 46-mile railroad and operated 19 grain elevators with a storage capacity of 20 million bushels.

The first country elevators were made from stacked wood planks nailed flat and faced with galvanized iron or tin sheeting. A 20,000-bushel wood elevator could be constructed for about $4,000. By the 1920s, as harvests grew and the price of grain topped one dollar per bushel, larger elevators were built from poured-in-place concrete. They were expensive but more durable.

One method of accumulating the capital needed to invest in elevators was a co-op where each farm family in an area bought a share of stock and had one vote in how the stored grain was bought and sold. After Oklahoma's first co-op grain elevator was built in Elk City in 1905, the number grew to 36 in 1913 and 91 in 1937, when co-ops handled 36 percent of the state wheat crop.

Shawnee Mills
(OHS)

Cathedrals of the Plains

In 1919, when Oklahoma farmers harvested a record 66 million bushels of wheat, there were 866 country elevators in the state with a storage capacity of 17 million bushels. The key to moving that grain from farm to market was a handful of terminal elevators, often referred to as cathedrals of the plains.

One of the first entrepreneurs to recognize that emerging market was W. B. Johnston, a former school teacher who made the land run of 1893 and started a coal and feed business in Enid. In 1910 he invested in a 40,000-bushel grain elevator and eventually expanded to 32 elevators in the region. His grandson Lew Meibergen added to that success. He bought the company in 1976 and built a 50,000-bushel-per-hour shuttle train, a trucking company, five seed-cleaning facilities, an experimental farm, and water ports in two states. By 2014 his terminal elevators in Enid could store more than 20 million bushels of wheat.

Milling added another layer of value to grain elevators as wheat went from farm to market. In 1906, when Oklahoma had 50 mills grinding an average of 7,000 barrels of flour per day, a young man who had been a flour salesman and manager for a candy company bought a small mill in Shawnee. That man was J. Lloyd Ford and his renamed firm was the Shawnee Milling Company. Three generations of the Ford family would prosper by taking additional risks during an era of consolidation. They rebuilt and modernized their mills after fires in 1934 and 1954.

Johnston Elevator, c. 1980 (OHS)

In 1964, responding to demand for convenience in the kitchen, they started selling packaged baking mixes. By 2015, when there were only four mills operating in Oklahoma, Shawnee Mills had two of them and employed more than 200 people.

Superior Feed

Superior Feed Mills, whose radio jingle started with the line "Get up and feed those chickens before they raise the dickens," was rebranded in 1929 by Kamil and B. D. Eddie, the two sons of Diab and Mary Salaum Eid, immigrants who had come to Oklahoma from their native Lebanon. Their first enterprise, a grocery store converted to a feed store, relocated to Stockyards City and then moved to South Robinson in downtown Oklahoma City. The Eddies added vitamins and cod liver oil to their chicken feed and opened their own nutritionist-run laboratory. By the 1940s Superior Feed was the state's biggest wholesaler of livestock feed with outlets in Oklahoma, Kansas, and Texas.

Superior feed sack
(OHS)

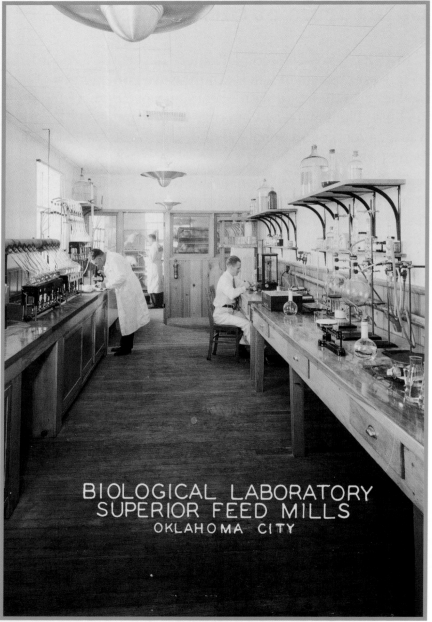

Superior Feed laboratory
(OHS)

Progress Beer

In 1892 a small elevator in Yukon was purchased by two Czechoslovakian families, the Kroutils and Dobrys. They called their new enterprise Yukon Mill and Grain Company. By the 1930s the mill was processing up to 2,000 barrels of Yukon's Best Flour per day with storage capacity for more than one million bushels of grain. John Kroutil found other ways to add value to grain.

He founded the Yukon National Bank so farmers could plant their crops, and he founded the Progress Beer Company after Congress repealed Prohibition in 1934. From 1959 to 1974, the 3.2 beer was bottled under the Lone Star Beer brand.

Tap room of Progress Beer, John Kroutils far right
(Mary D. Streich)

Installing telephone lines next to the Palace Drug Store, McAlester, IT., March 17, 1907 (OHS)

Taking a Risk

The value added to cattle, hogs, cotton, corn, and wheat flowed back into Oklahoma's economy and blended with oil dollars to stimulate investment in businesses that could compete in the marketplace. Living in a landlocked state where distance was an obstacle to be overcome, it was no surprise that Oklahoma businessmen earned success in transportation and communication. All it took was a willingness to take a risk and the business partners to provide the money to get started.

S.W. Bell Telephone
Building, Oklahoma City
(OHS)

Pioneer Telephone

John M. Noble
(OHS)

John M. Noble, a native of Kansas who had earned a college degree in electrical engineering, moved to Pawnee in 1897 with a plan to start a telephone company. He and his partners borrowed $2,200 and built a long distance toll line from Pawnee to Perry to Stillwater. They called it the Arkansas Valley Telephone Company.

Five years later Noble and his partners moved their headquarters to Oklahoma City, which was about to become the fastest growing city in the nation, and changed the name of the company to Pioneer Telephone and Telegraph. After a series of acquisitions on the eve of statehood, they were successful enough to build the first Chicago-style skyscraper in the Twin Territories, a seven-story limestone structure located at 3rd and Broadway. They called it the Pioneer Building.

In 1917 Pioneer merged with several other long distance carriers to create Southwestern Bell Telephone, a subsidiary affiliated with Alexander Graham Bell's American Telephone and Telegraph. Within a decade Southwestern Bell represented an investment of more than $30 million, making it one of the largest corporations in the young state with 5,176 people on the payroll, including 3,647 women.

Switchboard Operators, 1920
(OHS)

Investors Take Flight

Oklahomans embraced the risky new frontier of aviation. Not only were the potential rewards high, but the opportunity to get from here to there faster than anything possible before was enticing to a community that seemed to be far from every other place.

In 1911 an automobile dealer in Enid built an airplane from plans and started tinkering with a new design he tested on the Great Salt Plains. When he could not convince local bankers to invest, he went to Wichita, Kansas, where he started his business. His name was Clyde Cessna, the one who got away.

The boldest investors were oilmen who lived in a world of high risks, deep pockets, and intense competition to promote aviation fuel. William G. Skelly, a successful oilman in Tulsa, purchased a small aviation company in 1928 and renamed it Spartan Aircraft. His first product was a sturdy biplane, but he gained fame with the Spartan Executive, a sleek corporate plane that set speed records.

F. C. Hall, an oilman in Chickasha, bought a Lockheed Vega and hired a one-eyed pilot to push the limits of speed and distance. The airplane, named for Hall's daughter, was the Winnie Mae and the pilot was Wiley Post.

Clyde Cessna's first plane
(OHS)

Wiley Post
and Harold Gatty
(OHS)

Braniff Airlines

Paul Braniff, who was three years old when his father moved to Oklahoma City in 1900, stepped onto the stage of aviation history with bravado. While his older brother Thomas expanded the family insurance business, Paul learned to fly during World War I, earned his pilot's license, and flew with a touring air show in the 1920s. In 1928, with financing from his brother and two oilmen from Chickasha, he bought a Stinson Detroiter for $11,000 and started Braniff Airlines as the first regularly scheduled air service in the state.

As the sole pilot, Paul made three round trips a day from Oklahoma City to Tulsa. Passengers paid $12.50 for a one-way ticket or $20 for a round trip. That first year, the fledgling airline carried more than 3,000 passengers. He bought additional airplanes, most carrying five to six passengers, and hired pilots at a salary of $300 a month. In 1929, after merging with another company and expanding routes to Dallas and Fort Worth, Paul Braniff purchased two six-passenger Lockheed Vegas, the fastest ships in the air.

The Great Depression pushed Braniff Airlines to the brink of bankruptcy by 1934. Unable to raise money and $40,000 in debt, Paul Braniff won an airmail contract that saved the company. Under the deal, the U.S. Postal Service would pay Braniff 22.5 cents per air mile to transport 35 cubic feet of mail. For the route from Dallas to Chicago, the extra income of $180 kept his planes in the air. Within four years Braniff was flying 20 schedules to 15 cities. After opening a new operations base at Dallas's Love Field in 1941, Braniff moved company headquarters there in 1942.

Paul Braniff
(OHS)

Wiley Post Hangar

In 1928 the Curtiss-Wright Corporation invested $115,000 in an airfield north of Oklahoma City near a new housing addition called Nichols Hills. The most prominent structure was a hangar built with metal trusses and sliding doors. Four years later the hangar was leased to two men. One was Wiley Post, who worked on his beloved Winnie Mae under the trusses, and the other was Paul Braniff, whose Braniff Airlines fleet was based there from 1932 to 1935. The Wiley Post Hangar was saved from destruction many years later by a group of businessmen led by Jackie Cooper, Don Dennis, and Bill Anoatubby. In 2014 the surviving pieces of the hangar were donated to the Oklahoma Historical Society.

Inside of a
Kerr-McGee plane
(OHS)

Curtiss Wright Flying Service hangar, Bethany, 1935
(Paul Freeman)

Aero Commander

Like Paul and Thomas Braniff of an earlier era, brothers Rufe and Bill Amis pushed the frontiers of aviation higher, faster, and safer in the 1950s. The Amis family came to Oklahoma in 1934 to build roads. At first, they moved earth with the force of more than 150 mules. By the time they made the cut through the Arbuckle Mountains for Interstate 35, they used the world's largest tracked excavators. In 1950, after they helped build Oklahoma City's Downtown Airpark, they leaped at another chance to invest in their passion for airplanes. The object of their affection was the Aero Commander.

Based in a 26,000-square-foot hangar at Wiley Post Airport, the Aero Design and Engineering Company produced a string of celebrated aircraft throughout the 1950s. It started with Ted Smith's design of a twin-engine business airplane that was capable of taking off, flying, and landing with only one engine. After test pilots flew an Aero Commander from Oklahoma City to Washington D.C. with one propeller removed, the Air Force ordered 15 aircraft. Two of them were added to Air Force One for President Dwight D. Eisenhower.

An Aero Commander broke the distance record for general aviation in 1957 by flying a distance of 1,504 miles from Guatemala to Oklahoma. A year later, after building the first pressurized business aircraft in history, the Amis brothers and their partners sold the company to Rockwell Standard Aviation. The company went on to produce a series of aircraft with jet props and turbines while employing an average work force of more than 1,400 people. The last Aero Commander rolled off the assembly line in Oklahoma City in 1985.

Aero Commander
(OHS)

Aero Commander
(OHS)

Baron's Store, 400 W. Main, Oklahoma City, October 1945, (OHS)

Chapter Four

Cultivating Creativity

From 1930 to 1959, entrepreneurs found opportunities as more and more people moved from farms to cities and the world grew smaller through greater mobility, popular culture, and international trade. Armed with new technology, investors opened new markets, created new products, and drove the wheels of economic development in new directions despite the convulsions of the Great Depression and the dislocations of World War II.

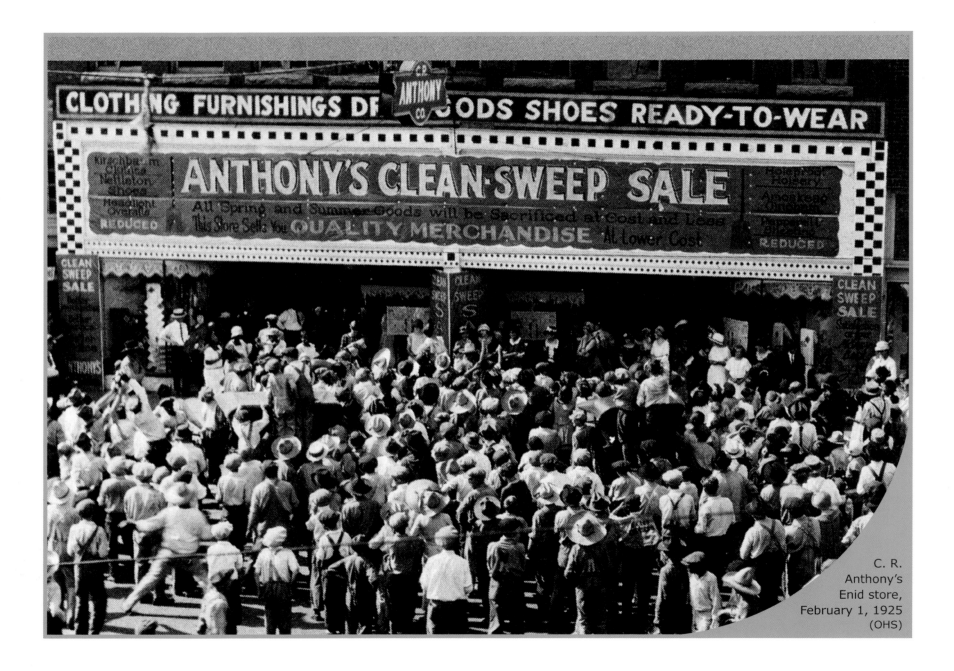

C. R. Anthony's Enid store, February 1, 1925 (OHS)

Cash and Carry

From 1930 to 1959 the traditional model of mom and pop general stores relying on high markups, low volume sales, and credit extended to neighbors finally gave way to a new generation of entrepreneurs who used high volume purchasing power, lower prices, and cash transactions. While some retailers grew through multiple stores, others found their own niche in the market place.

B. C. Clark Jewelers, across from John A. Brown's, Oklahoma City (OHS)

Regional Giants

Despite the uncertain times of the Great Depression, a few retail merchants in Oklahoma assumed greater risks and expanded from their small town roots.

C. R. Anthony launched his enterprise in 1922 when he opened his first clothing store with $10,000 in merchandise. Within a year he had stores in six small oil boom towns: Cushing, Pawhuska, Hominy, Barnsdall, Anadarko, and Chickasha. Keys to his success included a motived management team, with each store manager becoming a one-third owner, and an aggressive business plan that mixed seasonal sales, one-day events, and regional advertising with strict accountability. Many baby boomers still remember the pneumatic tubes used to control cash transactions. By 1972 there were 325 C. R. Anthony's stores in 21 states west of the Mississippi River.

In 1936, just as the Great Depression was reaching its lowest point, three merchants in western Oklahoma created a new variety store

C. R. Anthony
(OHS)

called TG&Y. The founders--Rawdon Tomlinson of Frederick, Enoch Gosselin of Cordell, and Raymond Young of Kingfisher—gained an advantage over competitors by pooling their resources into what they called the Central Merchandise Corporation, a giant warehouse operation in Oklahoma City where they could purchase inventory directly from manufacturers and bypass wholesalers. By 1980 the TG&Y chain included 930 stores. Two young men who recognized the efficiency of that operation were Sam Walton, a native of Kingfisher and the future founder of Walmart, and David Green, who worked at TG&Y and went on to found Hobby Lobby.

Sam Walton
(OHS)

David Green
(OHS)

All in the Family

Growth and volume sales were not the only strategies for surviving hard times. Sometimes it was taking advantage of opportunities to enhance what families know best.

W. W. Starr founded Starr Lumber Company in Alva in 1909. While expanding his string of lumber yards to 14 small communities in northwest Oklahoma, Starr built homes where oil or agriculture created a demand. In 1944, just as small town lumberyards started to struggle, ownership passed to Starr's son-in-law, Norman Ryerson, who spent the next decade closing the smaller yards. Starr's grandson, Richard Ryerson, took the reins in 1960 and completed the transformation but refused to give up. He consolidated and expanded operations in four communities—Alva, Woodward, Blackwell, and Enid—where there were enough people to respond to his brand of customer service. His son John, who became manager in 1999, built on his family legacy when he assumed the risk of rehabilitating a historic hotel on the town square in Alva.

Louis "Bummy" Sharpe Jr. opened Sharpe's Dry Goods in Checotah in 1913. During the following decades he expanded to 12 stores, including one in Norman, two in Tulsa, and two in Oklahoma City. Leadership of the company passed to his

Starr Lumber
(Ryerson Family)

son Louis Sharpe III and to his grandsons, Louis Sharpe IV and Logan Sharpe, who closed the urban stores and returned to their small town roots. Like C. R. Anthony had done, the Sharpes retained a basic business plan that included profit sharing for all employees and matched low volume sales with low overhead by keeping their headquarters in Checotah. They also matched personal service with innovations. During the savings and loan crisis of the 1980s, the Sharpes aggressively bid on merchandise being liquidated in bankruptcies. Special stores were opened for perpetual "clearance sales." They also added basic dental care through partnerships with dentists who had skills but little capital for offices and staff support. By 2015 there were 24 Sharpe's Department Stores in Oklahoma, Arkansas, and Louisiana.

Creating a Niche

While retail merchants found innovative ways to keep costs low and sales high, other innovators created products that filled a niche in the market.

An artist-turned-businessman who created his own opportunity was John Frank, a professor of ceramic arts at the University of Oklahoma. In 1934, as folk art gained popularity in the market place, Frank established a business to produce high quality pottery that was both decorative and useful. He called the firm Frankoma. Initially using beige-colored clay dug near Ada, Frank created a wide variety of molded pottery, including the popular Wagon Wheel dinnerware and the seasonal Christmas plates. In 1938 he and his wife Grace moved the company to Sapulpa, where they discovered red clay that became the base for their pottery after 1954. Today, even though the factory is closed, Frankoma pottery still generates commercial value as highly collectible folk art.

In 1949 a young inventor named Jasper "R. D." Hull pitched a novel idea to managers at the Zero Hour Bomb Company in Tulsa. After being inspired by the way a butcher pulled twine off a spool, he built an enclosed fishing reel that eliminated tangles. Faced with declining sales of their oil field products, the officials at the Zero Hour Bomb Company took a chance and fabricated a line of fishing reels using the shortened version of their

Frankoma Pottery trimmers, 1956 (OHS)

company name-- Zebco. Within five years the Zebco 33, selling at a retail price of $19.95, gained national fame and made Zebco an industry leader. By the time of Hull's death in 1977, he held 35 patents for 26 reel designs and Zebco had sold more than 70 million reels.

Zebco advertisement (Oklahoma Department of Wildlife Conservation)

OTASCO

Sam, Maurice, and Herman Sanditen were Lithuanian Jewish immigrants working as mechanics in South Carolina when they heard about the oil booms in Oklahoma. They moved west, opened a garage, and started selling automobile supplies in Okmulgee shortly after World War I. They called their business Oklahoma Tire & Supply, OTASCO for short. Initially they specialized in selling gasoline, tires, and automotive accessories, but out of necessity expanded to consumer products such as vacuum cleaners, radios, appliances, and toys during the 1930s. They also franchised the OTASCO brand to independent owners and served as the exclusive wholesaler. By 1959 the Sanditen family operated 86 stores and supplied another 167 franchised locations.

B. C. Clark business card, Indian Territory
(OHS)

B. C. Clark Jewelers

B. C. Clark opened his first jewelry store in Purcell, Indian Territory, in 1892. As the little town grew, he added merchandise ranging from player pianos and radios to refrigerators and automobiles. In 1929 he moved to downtown Oklahoma City and returned to what he did best—jewelry. The strategy paid off during the Great Depression when he carved out a niche by selling pocket watches to railroad employees with installment payments deducted from their payroll checks. The founder was joined in the business by his son, B. C. Clark Jr., and grandson, Jim Clark. In 1957, following their customers into the post-war suburbs, they opened a store in the Mayfair Shopping Center and expanded radio and television advertising with a catchy jingle. A third store was moved to Penn Square Mall in 1988. Today, led by the fourth generation, the Clarks and their staff are doing what they know best.

OTASCO, ca. 1945
(OHS)

Oliver's Shoe Stores

Charlie Oliver moved to Woodward in 1929 to take a job as an assistant manager of a C. R. Anthony's store. Four years later, at one of the lowest points of the Great Depression, he quit his secure job and started his own retail operation. He called it Oliver's Shoe Store. Like his former boss, he expanded to other towns in the region, with stores in Guymon, Enid, Norman, Moore, Ardmore, Altus, Cushing, Larned and Liberal, Kansas, and Perryton and Abilene, Texas. Willing to take risks, he added women's ready-made clothing to the store in Woodward and invested in a housing addition on the west side of Woodward in 1959.

Elks Rodeo Parade in Woodward, October 15, 1936 (OHS)

Women trying on shoes, 1942
(*LIFE* magazine)

Stock Exchange Bank

In 1912 a young man from Arkansas was named cashier and manager of a country bank in Fargo, Oklahoma. The start-up financial institution was the Stock Exchange Bank and the young man's name was A. M. Benbrook. A decade later, he bought the bank and served the first generation of farmers and ranchers on the land. In 1939, after surviving the financial melt-down of the Great Depression, Benbrook merged with a bank in Sharon and moved the Stock Exchange Bank to Woodward. His son, Temple Benbrook, became president of the bank in 1965, followed by his son, Bruce Benbrook, who became president in 1981. Under family leadership, the Stock Exchange Bank was the only local bank to survive the banking crisis of the 1980s and has since grown through a commitment to community service.

The bank sign is a symbol of perseverance. It was installed at the bank in 1947 after a deadly tornado killed more than 200 people and destroyed much of the commercial district. Bruce Benbrook donated the sign to the Oklahoma Historical Society in 2002.

Stock Exchange Bank sign in the *Crossroads of Commerce* exhibit (OHS)

Highway
construction, 1939
(OHS)

Route 66 bypass, Oklahoma City, 1954
(OHS)

Mobility and Money

Greater mobility on a growing network of highways affected every sector of the economy from 1930 to 1959. In the world of retail sales, delivery by truck opened opportunities for bulk purchasing and regional distribution. In the world of popular culture, travel by automobile expanded the audience for movies, concerts, and dances. Meanwhile, the sale and service of trucks and automobiles created new opportunities for investors in every community of the state. For Oklahoma businessmen and women, mobility meant money.

From Here to There

Commerce had always depended on transportation, whether it was in wagons, riverboats, or trains, but the most revolutionary change in the history of getting goods and people from here to there emerged from the 1920s to the 1950s. It was the rise of the modern highway system.

The demand for highways erupted almost overnight. In 1907 there were fewer than 5,000 cars and trucks in Oklahoma. By 1926 the number exceeded 500,000 vehicles, including 25,000 trucks. Congress responded to this national trend in 1916 by providing matching grants for highway construction, but the State of Oklahoma did not act until 1923 when a one-penny-per-gallon tax was added to gasoline sales with all revenue used to match federal grants. From 1924 to 1930 the miles of paved roadway in Oklahoma soared from 227 to 3,368, including a new highway called Route 66.

One businessman who took advantage of the new highway system was Doane Farr. In 1919 Farr borrowed $7,000 to buy a half interest in the Clinton Transfer and Storage Company. The little company included short-haul delivery of wholesale groceries, coal, and ice to businesses in and around Clinton. In 1929, when the State of Oklahoma first regulated trucking, Farr purchased a Class A Permit to haul goods from Oklahoma City to the Texas border and a Class B Permit to haul general

Lee Way Freight
(OHS)

goods from Clinton to various points in the state. Despite the Great Depression, he bought another 16 short-line permits during the 1930s until he served 84 towns with 83 employees and 60 pieces of equipment. In 1945 he consolidated his holdings with three other trucking companies, including the intrastate routes of LeeWay Freight, into Sooner Federated Trucking. Each expansion, each new mile of highway made it easier for businessmen and women to get their goods and services from here to there.

Clinton Transfer
(OHS)

King of the Road

Bob Wills (OHS)

Better highway transportation combined with the new medium of radio to create an opportunity for a young entrepreneur who happened to play music that made people want to dance. The music was western swing and the man with the fiddle was Bob Wills.

Raised in the cotton fields of the Red River Valley, Bob Wills learned to play the fiddle from his father and combined country jigs, reels, and waltzes with the soulful sounds of gospel, blues, and jazz in what eventually would be called western swing. As with all gifted musicians, the challenge was how to make a living doing what he did best. For Bob, it was using the power of radio to fill dance halls where he performed with his band. In 1934, looking for a new base of operations with a powerful radio station and good access to the growing network of paved highways, Bob Wills and his band moved to Tulsa where he found his opportunity along Route 66.

The key to his subsequent success was radio station KVOO, 1170 on the AM dial, with 50,000 watts of broadcasting power that had already boosted the careers of Otto Gray and the Oklahoma Cowboys, Jimmie Wilson and his Catfish Band, and Gene Autry. William G. Skelly, the oilman who owned the station, gave Bob Wills the coveted time slot from 12:15 to 1:30 p.m. six days a week. The band

Playboy Flour (OHS)

secured a sponsor, the Red Star Milling Company, which created a new line of products called Play Boy Flour and Play Boy Bread. Purchases came with a trading card featuring one band member on the front and a recipe on the back. With a sponsor, a hit radio show, and a new fleet of 1937 Buicks to get them down the road, Bob Wills and the Texas Playboys filled dance halls across the region.

Dance to the Music

From 1934 to 1942 the Bob Wills radio show was broadcast daily from a former garage converted into a dance hall. The location would eventually be called the Brady Arts District of Tulsa and the name of the iconic landmark was Cain's.

The story began with Tate Brady, a native of Missouri who moved into the Creek Nation in 1890. As an intermarried citizen of the Cherokee Nation, he helped incorporate the city of Tulsa, built a hotel, and constructed a Hupmobile garage a few blocks north of the central business district in 1924. Six years later, Brady's heirs leased the garage to Madison "Daddy" Cain, who added a neon sign with animated dancers and charged ten cents for a dance lesson. He called the enterprise Cain's Dance Academy.

By 1937 Brady's heirs leased Cain's to O. W. Mayo, the business manager for western swing pioneer Bob Wills. Mayo bought the building in 1944 and leased it to different promoters, including Bob Wills, who brought in groups playing popular music of the era. Then came troubled times as musical tastes changed, repeal of prohibition added age restrictions, and the surrounding neighborhood deteriorated. In 1976, when the building was sold to Larry Shaeffer, Cain's had a brief revival hosting nontraditional acts such as the Sex Pistols. The comeback gained momentum after 2003 when Dr. James Rodgers took advantage of historic preservation efforts and a renewed interest in live music performed in an intimate setting. By 2015 Cain's once again was a venue for live music and an iconic asset in the world of popular culture.

Bob Wills and his Texas Playboys onstage performing at Cain's, c. 1940 (OHS)

Cain's Ballroom, Tulsa (OHS)

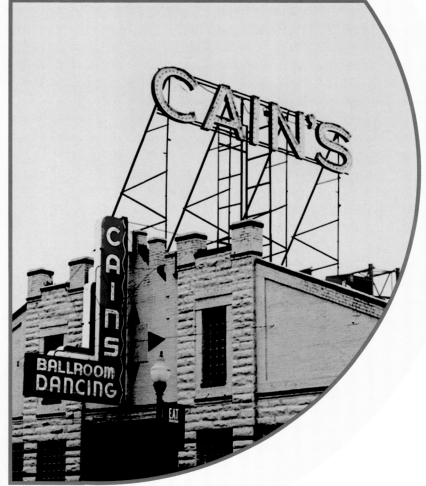

Oklahoma City, 1942
(OHS)

Emerging Markets

Digging out from the rubble of the Great Depression, Oklahoma's economy shifted course again after World War II as full employment and technological advances opened new doors of opportunity. Some of the impact was a direct result of military spending, while the greater impact was provided by investors who created businesses and tapped new markets.

Around 36th Street and Pennsylvania Avenue, Oklahoma City, 1947 (OHS)

The Winds of War

For Oklahoma and the United States, World War II was a political, social, and economic turning point. While sons and fathers fought on distant battlefields, folks on the home front pulled together to increase the production of goods and services needed to win the war.

One Oklahoma-based company tested by the winds of war was Manhattan Construction, founded by Laurence H. Rooney in 1896. From territorial roots in Chandler, the Rooney family moved headquarters to Muskogee and grew the company into a regional giant specializing in county courthouses, schools, and instant landmarks such as the First National Bank Building in Oklahoma City. The company tenaciously survived the Great Depression and was prepared when the country needed new infrastructure as war approached. First came several base expansions from Illinois to Colorado, followed by the construction of the Douglas Bomber Plant in Tulsa in the summer of 1941. Manhattan's greatest challenge was Camp Gruber, an infantry training base 15 miles east of Muskogee that included relocation of a state highway, the construction of 1,731 buildings, and the reproduction of a northern European landscape with roads, fields, fences, and hedgerows. All of the work was completed in only four months. For its efforts, Manhattan Construction was awarded the coveted E Pennant. Still guided by the Rooney family in 2015,

CAMP HEADQUARTERS, CAMP GRUBER

SIG. C., U. S. ARMY

Camp Gruber
(OHS)

Manhattan has earned an international reputation for taking on big challenges such as Cowboy Stadium in Arlington, Texas, the U. S. Capitol Visitor Center in Washington, D.C., and the Oklahoma History Center.

The Douglas Bomber Plant built by Manhattan Construction in Tulsa was re-tasked after the war. In a deal negotiated by the Tulsa Chamber of Commerce, the people of Tulsa invested bond money to retrofit the hangars into a maintenance center for American Airlines, which was led by a native of Oklahoma named Red Mosier. To design the facilities, American Airlines hired a new architectural and engineering firm just formed in Oklahoma City. Today, that firm is known as FSB, Frankfort-Short-Bruza, a national leader in the design of aviation facilities. In 2015 the American Airline Maintenance and Worldwide Reservation Center in Tulsa was still one of the largest civilian employers in the state.

Bricks and Mortar

After World War I the fastest growing segment of Oklahoma's economy was housing, a result of population growth, installment loans made possible by the newly created Federal Reserve, and balloon construction techniques that lowered prices and encouraged mass production in big housing developments.

One of the most aggressive Oklahoma entrepreneurs taking advantage of this opportunity was G. A. "Doc" Nichols. A former dentist, Nichols created a vertical business model during the 1920s that included lumberyards, architects, construction crews, realtors, and a savings and loan. His first big developments included many of the historic preservation districts in Oklahoma City, but his boldest investment was Nichols Hills, launched in 1928 with more than 2,000 acres of land, landscaping, riding trails, golf course, and airport. Some of Oklahoma City's wealthiest families, such as John A. Brown, E. K. Gaylord, and Frank Buttram led the way by building grand mansions. When the Great Depression pushed Nichols to the brink of bankruptcy, First National Bank's Charles Vose confidently restructured his loans and kept the developer's dreams alive. Nichols Hills would set the pace for upscale housing well into the 21st century.

In 1937, while Doc Nichols was clinging to solvency, a family on the other side of the tracks was doubling down and investing in housing of a

Edwards Housing Addition (Johnson Family)

different sort. The developers were Walter J. and Frances Edwards, African American pioneers who have been called "serial entrepreneurs." Their story starts in 1915 when the 22-year-old Edwards started working in a junkyard making nine dollars a week. He saved, bought a horse and wagon, and opened businesses that included carpet cleaning, an ice cream plant, taxi cabs, service stations, pharmacies, and his own salvage yard. In 1930 he married Frances, who became an active partner. In 1937 they purchased 33 acres of undeveloped land between NE 10th and NE 16th streets along Grand Boulevard and started building homes. By 1939, after earning the first FHA (Federal Housing Administration) loan guarantees for an African American housing addition, they expanded to 170 acres and more than 800 homes. The Edwards family donated land for a park, school, and church, then built a hospital that would treat patients regardless of the color of a person's skin. The Edwards's legacy included home ownership, jobs, and a greater sense of community.

Character Counts

Despite a glut of imported crude and low prices, the oil industry remained a vital part of Oklahoma's economy as the country emerged from World War II. One result of the retrenchment was a shift from exploration and drilling to greater efficiencies and reduced operating costs. Creating his own niche during this time of change was the innovative genius Garman Kimmell.

Born in Maryland and raised in Kansas, Kimmell came to Oklahoma to study petroleum engineering at the University of Oklahoma. He completed his master's degree in 1937 and served as chief of research at a local firm for the next 11 years. In 1948 he started his own company, Kimray, Inc., in Oklahoma City with four employees. His big breakthrough was a small but efficient product that revolutionized the way high pressure gas was regulated both upstream and downstream. It was called the 3-Inch SGT-BP.

In 1956 Kimray moved into a 12,000-square-foot building where Kimmell merged his inventiveness with a highly refined sense of organizational efficiency. He plotted cash flow and work production, instilled a workplace value system based on integrity, and turned out a succession of new products such as a liquid level control system, a low pressure release valve, and a revolutionary energy exchange glycol pump that changed the way the oil and gas industry

Garman O. Kimmel, President of Kimray, Inc., 1986 (OHS)

removed moisture from natural gas. By the time of his death, Kimmell held 28 patents and had served 57 years as what he called "chief developer."

Oil field equipment was only part of Kimmell's contribution to Oklahoma. He invented a wide range of mechanical devices, such as the Vena-Cava Filter used in more than a half million open heart surgeries, a line of high fidelity music components, and a folding apparatus to treat patients suffering from back pain. He also excelled as a community volunteer. He taught Sunday school for 60 years, started the Character Training Institute, and tithed ten percent of company profits to church and charity. In 2015, with annual sales exceeding $240 million, Kimmell's son-in-law Tom Hill and grandson Thomas Hill announced plans to move the still growing company to a new campus north of town. As Garman Kimmell demonstrated through a life of creativity, character counts.

Helicopters on the High Plains

The future of general aviation looked bright as the nation recovered from World War II. On the high plains of western Oklahoma, where distance was something to be conquered, personal ownership of airplanes and helicopters was especially appealing, but there were not enough local customers to support a business. One innovator who found a way to bridge his love of flight with a career was Wayne Kinzie.

Kinzie learned to fly while still at Alva High School. After starting college at Northwestern State, he bought two wrecked airplanes and combined the parts into one that could fly. He started a lawn mower and bicycle repair business after graduation, but kept dabbling with aircraft. In 1951, realizing he had found a niche in the market place, he created Kinzie Industries to salvage, repair, and service airplanes fulltime. He soon was renting space at the Alva Airport from the Alva Industrial Foundation and pulling a trailer around the country picking up wrecked airplanes.

Kinzie reached a turning point in 1961. He married his wife, Beverly, who added organizational and bookkeeping skills to the enterprise. That same year he salvaged his first helicopter. He repaired it, and in typical pioneer fashion, flew the rebuilt contraption to Tulsa to take flying lessons. After Kinzie Industries became a certified repair station for Hughes helicopters, the famous underwater

Wayne Kinzie
(Kinzie Family)

explorer Jacques Cousteau came to Alva to retrofit a helicopter that could operate off the deck of the Calypso.

Son Paul Kenzie started working with his father and mother while still a child. By the time he graduated from Northwestern, he was ready to expand the business. He completed mechanical drawings for parts, learned to recover wrecked aircraft from remote locations, and earned the confidence of his father who once told him to learn how to fabricate parts from a plastics extruder. In 1999 the plastics fabrication division of Kinzie Industries became a separate company called Plane Plastics. As the Kinzie family proved, there was room on the high plains for helicopters.

Creativity in the Trenches

As opposed to the Great Depression, when labor intensive projects were needed to reduce unemployment, the post war economy rewarded innovators who improved efficiencies through technology and reduced labor costs. Ed Malzahn was a master at both.

Malzahn was born into a family of innovators. His grandfather Carl Malzahn came from Germany and established a blacksmith shop in the farming community of Perry. His father, Charles, converted the business to a machine shop as oil play came into the county. Ed learned the arts of metal work and machines, but added to his skill sets with a mechanical engineering degree from Oklahoma A&M (now OSU).

His first inventions were targeted for the oil industry. He designed and built a portable drilling rig, but could not raise the money to go into production. He designed and built a simple device called a Geronimo that derrick workers could use to escape rig disasters. He then found his true calling after he saw a plumber hand-digging a trench from the city water main to a house under construction. How, he thought, could he build a durable, one-person power trencher that was small enough to get through a gate yet affordable enough for a small plumbing contractor? In 1948, after two years working on design and fabrication, Ed Malzahn demonstrated what was eventually called the Ditch Witch.

Ten years and much work later, the inventor borrowed $140,000 from the First National Bank of Perry to build a small plant in his hometown. To honor his father, he called the company Charles Machine Works. Then, instead of simply selling his trenchers through retail outlets, he developed a network of independent dealers focused on his line of machinery with a central corps of sales representatives who spent two weeks of every month in the field working with customers and two weeks in the plant working on new products. By 2015 Ditch Witch dealers were on every continent except Africa and Antartica with an average workforce exceeding 1,000 employees in Perry.

Early Ditch Witch assembly plant (Ditch Witch)

Celebrating with a Bang

A few short years after World War II, Norman V. Burnett made a fateful decision that would drive his professional life for the next half century. In 1948 he established Burnett Fireworks, a fifteen acre facility near Enid, Oklahoma.

Burnett recognized the post-war presence of pent up desire of American consumers to celebrate traditional and special events. War-time frugality had ended, and American consumers had new-found disposable income to spend on special purchases like fireworks. Barnett was there to fill that need.

Originally Burnett's company specialized in Class C consumer fireworks. But by 1952 his business plan had changed. He purchased Denver-based Western Fireworks and changed the company name to Western Enterprises, Inc. The company vision and mission also expanded to include the sale of Class B fireworks with a regional market encompassing Oklahoma, Colorado, Kansas, and New Mexico.

During the 1950s as Burnett's company grew, it also carved out a market niche, perfecting the art of set piece design and developing animation devices for movement and theatrical presentation during fireworks displays. Burnett's son Jim joined his father in developing these business innovations.

By the late 1970s, Western Enterprises, now under the direction of Jim Burnett, made the strategic decision to focus solely on Class B Public Display Fireworks, discontinuing its Class C consumer division. Innovations continued. Fireworks choreography was introduced and perfected. A 300 position electronic firing system was created.

Western Enterprises would gain loyal customers and widespread acclaim for its work, both nationally and internationally. On November 16, 2007, Western Enterprise produced the grand fireworks finale for the Oklahoma Centennial Celebration. Similar extravaganzas were produced in cities such as Quebec City and Vancouver, Canada.

From its humble beginnings to its current international success, Western Enterprises, Inc., still maintains its headquarters near Enid, Oklahoma.

by Tim Zwink

Oklahoma Centennial
Celebration, 2007
(Western Enterprises)

Oklahoma
Livestock and
Rodeo Show, 1946
(OHS)

Dividends of Cowboy Culture

Oklahoma businessmen and women have long recognized the commercial value of cowboy culture. After the popularity of Wild West Shows faded in the 1920s and 1930s, public demand for anything cowboy was satisfied through music, movies, television shows, and rodeo. Some businessmen taking advantage of this opportunity were performers while others were ranchers and workaday cowboys using skills earned through time in the saddle.

Cowboy and cowgirls at Allen's shoe store, Oklahoma City
(OHS)

Reel Cowboys

In 1903 W. D. Griffith released his first full-length feature film, *The Great Train Robbery*. It was a huge financial success. Soon, film makers were looking for cowboys who could ride a horse, shoot a gun, rope a steer, and look the part of a rugged frontiersman. They found them in Oklahoma.

By 1929 each of the "Famous Foursome" of silent-era cowboy movie stars had roots in Oklahoma. Ken Maynard, Buck Jones, Hoot Gibson, and Tom Mix started their careers on the Miller Brothers' 101 Ranch, where they worked as cowboys, competed in rodeos, and performed in the famous Wild West Shows. Gibson won the All-Around World Championship title in 1912, while Mix earned the attention of movie makers when he rode a blind-folded horse off a cliff. At the peak of their careers, Gibson made $14,500 a week, while Mix made $17,500 a week. Their spending helped drive the wheels of the economy wherever they happened to be at any given time.

The financial success of westerns continued into the "talkie" era as another generation of cowboys from Oklahoma hit the big screen. Gene Autry, who grew up on a ranch near Ravia, was discovered by Will Rogers in the little town of Chelsea where Autry was working as a telegraph operator. Encouraged by the Cherokee movie star, Autry moved to New York City in 1925 to perform on radio and made his

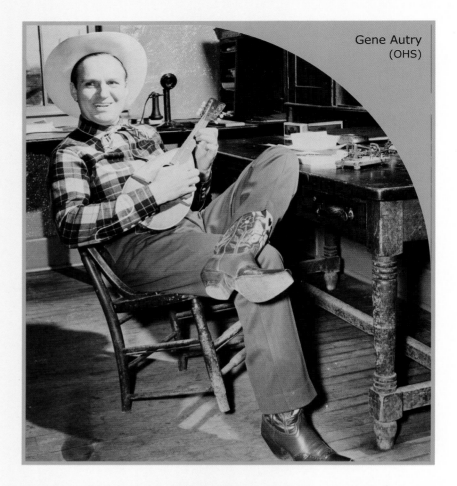

Gene Autry
(OHS)

first movie with Ken Maynard in 1934. As a savvy businessman, Autry made 93 movies, released 635 records, performed on the hit radio series *Melody Ranch*, and became the first cowboy movie star to jump to a regularly scheduled television show in 1950. By the time of his death in 1998 the movie star-turned-businessman owned a string of radio and television stations, a huge ranch in Oklahoma, and the California Angels baseball team.

(Rennard Strickland Collection)

Lead, Zinc, and the Silver Screen

As cowboy culture added to the popularity of movies in the 1920s and 1930s, Oklahoma businessmen invested in theaters. Most theaters outside of Oklahoma City and Tulsa were small, unadorned buildings, but a few achieved a high style of architectural exuberance. One of the most opulent was the Coleman Theatre in the little town of Miami, Oklahoma, and the man with the checkbook was George Coleman.

Coleman was a water well digger in northeastern Oklahoma who made a fortune mining lead and zinc along the southwestern flank of the Ozark Plateau. During World War I, 50 percent of the zinc and 45 percent of the lead needed for the war effort came from Ottawa County, and much of that was mined by Coleman's company. With his fortune made, he decided to build a theater so his employees and neighbors could enjoy stage acts and movies. He cut no corners. The ornate exterior was Spanish Revival with gargoyle-like creatures gazing down from the cornice. Inside, he installed central heating and cooling, used dimmer boards with magnetic controls to provide lighting effects, and purchased a brand new Wurlitzer organ. With seating for 1,600 people and tickets selling for $1, he opened the theatre on April 18, 1929.

In 1989, when the theater was no longer contributing to the local economy, the Coleman family donated the aging relic to the people of Miami. Three years later the Friends of the Coleman launched a community-based effort to invest in its former glory. They organized work teams to clean pigeon droppings, repair plaster, and paint surfaces. They raised money to buy back and restore the original Wurlitzer organ and fabricated a replica of the original cut-glass chandelier. They started a seat-adoption program with 1,000 donors. By 2002 the Friends of the Coleman had invested more than 6 million volunteer hours and hundreds of thousands of dollars in the restoration project. Like George Coleman, the community took a risk and provided another asset to drive the economy.

The Coleman Theatre showing *Old Yeller*, 1959 (OHS)

Behind the Camera

The popularity of cowboy culture created opportunities for Oklahoma entrepreneurs who wanted to make movies. As if stepping out of the pages of frontier history, three U S marshals created a company to make movies in 1914. They were Bill Tilghman, E. D. Nix, and Chris Madsen.

All three lawmen were frustrated with the number of western movies that glorified outlaws. To offer a more realistic version of history, they created the Eagle Film Company and started assembling a team to make a movie called *The Passing of the Oklahoma Outlaw*. They hired a director and screenwriter from out of state, but found a

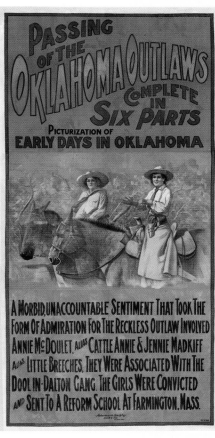

(Rennard Strickland)

photographer and "advisor" in Chandler, Oklahoma. His name was Bennie Kent, a native of England who had been making and selling newsreels for the growing movie industry since 1909.

Scenes were shot on the actual locations where gunfights, bank robberies, and arrests had occurred. When possible, lawmen and outlaws played themselves. The movie was distributed to theaters as a package deal. If the movie was booked, Tilghman or one of the lawmen in the movie would give a lecture about law and order. Tilghman made four movies with his pioneering film company before his life tragically ended in 1924. Ironically, the 70-year-old lawman was shot and killed in a gunfight on the streets of an oilfield boom town still fighting for law and order.

Chris Madsen and Bill Tilghman, (OHS)

109

Cowboy Competition

Behind the popular culture of movies and music were real cowboys and cowgirls who had been raised riding horses, roping cattle, and sharing the values of rugged individualism and hard work on the land. As the Great Depression and World War II pushed more and more rural folks to towns and cities, many real cowboys satisfied their love of ranch life through round-up clubs and cowboy competition.

By 1946 more than 10,000 Oklahomans belonged to 125 round-up clubs across the state. Each, in its own way, was a small business with investments, operating funds, and services. Typically, a club would build an arena and adjacent corrals where members could ride, rope, and compete against one another. In 1947 the Pawhuska Round-Up Club, with the support a new statewide magazine called *Oklahoma Roundup*, sponsored a competition called the International Cavalcade. Twelve events, scattered over three days, included bareback and saddle bronc riding, steer wrestling, team roping, calf roping, barrel racing, bull riding, and timed events that replicated skills used on the ranch. Entry was limited to the event champions of each round-up club. For the next seven decades, thousands of cowboys and cowgirls would descend on Pawhuska every summer for what would become the largest amateur rodeo event in the nation.

By the 1950s one of the most successful businesses serving cowboy culture was Beutler Brothers Rodeo Stock Company. With headquarters near Elk City, Oklahoma, the enterprise began in 1929 when three ranchers, brothers Jake, Lynn, and Elra Beutler, won a contract to supply the bucking stock for a rodeo in Canadian, Texas. They made $100 before expenses. Since then, Beutler Brothers and its successor company, Beutler & Son, have earned a reputation with cowboys and sponsors for the quality of their stock, including the Brahma bull Speck, which was ridden only once in 103 tries. The Beutlers also were innovators in adding entertainment value that included virtually every singing and acting star in Nashville and Hollywood. As the family has done every year for more than six decades, Beutler & Son had stock selected for the National Finals Rodeo in 2015.

Beutler Brothers Jake, Lynn and Elra
(OHS)

Round-up club
(OHS)

Cowboy Gear

From the 1930s to the 1950s the image of movie stars such as Gene Autry and Roy Rogers combined with the popularity of cowboy culture to create a growing market for saddles, bridles, boots, hats, and western wear. Oklahoma investors responded with manufacturing plants and retail stores.

George and Lovilla Trego entered the western wear business by accident. Their daughter, Thurlene, was selected as the first queen of the Woodward Elks Rodeo in 1934. She needed a special outfit, so they hired two women to sew a costume. The next step was creating Trego's Westwear Manufacturing. The Woodward-based company produced clothing for Neiman-Marcus in Dallas, but the best outlets were operated by the Trego family. Their daughter, Thurlene, and her husband, Garnett Frye, opened Frye's Old Town in Red River, New Mexico. Their son, Orlin, opened Trego's Men's Wear shops in Woodward and Cripple Creek, Colorado. Production and sales actually increased in the 1960s with the rise of a new, unexpected market for their fringed leather jackets, purses, and moccasins. Their new customers were hippies.

Trego's Westwear
(OHS)

One of the most famous saddle shops serving cowboys before World War II was Veach Saddlery of Trenton, Missouri. At the end of the war, Monroe Veach's daughter, Imogene, and her husband Charley Beals had $2,000 in savings to invest. They asked Monroe where they should open a saddle shop, and he said most of his custom orders were coming out of Oklahoma. On January 1, 1946, Charley and Imogene opened the Veach Saddlery Shop at the Tulsa Fairgrounds. While her husband earned an international reputation for saddles and his Charley Beals bareback riggings, Imogene completed the hand-tooling and designed western clothing. Their line of saddles and tack grew to include bits, spurs, polo and racing equipment, jeans, boots, and hats. The business would change locations several times, but it would remain a family operation. In 2015 Charley and Imogene's grandson, Drew Clark, was still running the Veach Saddlery Company from the family ranch located near Colcord, Oklahoma.

Advertisement for Veach Saddlery from *The Roundup*, February 1947 (OHS)

Hudiburg
Chevrolet, c. 1957
(Hudiburg Family)

Chapter Five

Chasing Consumers

From the 1960s to 1982, Oklahoma's economy reached a crossroads where cultural change intersected with dynamic innovation. As the Baby Boomers rolled through their teens and emerged as young adults, they and their parents created new markets for cars, food, recreation, and a wide range of consumer goods from hula hoops to hamburgers. It was the golden age of music, with top-ten radio and live television, a time for cruising Main Street and buying a first home.

Dairy Boy,
Fairview, 1958
(OHS)

Car Culture

The golden age of automobiles, when muscle cars shared the road with family station wagons, had a dramatic impact on Oklahoma's economy from 1960 to 1982. In addition to driving the suburban expansion of cities and generating demand for better highways, the new mobility created golden opportunities for entrepreneurs willing to take a risk.

The Rancher's Daughter Drive In,
4423 NW 23 Street, Oklahoma City,
May 1961
(OHS)

Mile of Cars

Fred Jones
(OHS)

Paul Hudiburg was a young man trying to avoid going back to the farm in 1945 when a banker asked him if he would assume ownership of a struggling car dealership in Prague, Oklahoma. When Hudiburg said he did not have any money, the banker said he would loan it to him. That was just the beginning. In 1957 Hudiburg purchased a promising Chevrolet dealership in Midwest City, a new suburban community shaped in large part by car culture, and eventually participated in creating more than 30 new dealerships across the state and region. David Hudiburg, cut from the same bolt of cloth as his father, became a general manager at the age of 22 and led another round of expansions. By 2015 the Hudiburg Auto Group employed more than 400 people at seven franchises.

In 1968 brothers Bill and Bob Doenges bought a Ford dealership in Tulsa from their father, Bill Doenges, a veteran in the industry who had started his career in towns such as Braman, Tonkawa, and Bartlesville. The Tulsa dealership faced several challenges. It was landlocked downtown with poor access and operations scattered in separate buildings. Willing to take a risk, Bill and Bob purchased 9.3 acres of land at 34th and S. Sheridan Road and started planning a suburban site accessible from a major highway. In 1974, just as the brothers retired their debt from the original purchase, they borrowed another $1.5 million and built the new dealership. Within two years it was the top-selling Ford dealership in Oklahoma.

With more than 40 years of experience selling and servicing cars and trucks, Fred Jones took a similar risk in 1968 and invested in the old Ford Assembly Plant located on the west edge of downtown Oklahoma City. The last Model A had rolled off the line in 1934, but the four-story building was perfect for Jones, who wanted to expand his parts remanufacturing operation to include transmissions and engines. In 1971 a workforce of more than 400 men and women at the Fred Jones Plant rebuilt more than 35,000 engines and shipped more than 1.5 million remanufactured parts to 2,500 Ford dealers from New Mexico to Florida.

Cars and Recreational Eating

The greater mobility provided by cars, combined with general prosperity and the increasing numbers of women entering the work force, created a growing demand for prepared meals that went beyond just eating to survive. In Oklahoma this intersection of cars and recreational eating encouraged investments in restaurants, cafeterias, and drive-ins.

In the early 1960s an official with the National Restaurant Association gave Oklahoma City the title of "Cafeteria Capital of the World." He was right. Oklahoma City had more than 32 cafeterias, some dating to the 1920s. Joe and Charlotte Dodson, both natives of Cordell, established the first cafeteria on the south side of town in 1952 when they invested $65,000 in equipment and furnishings in the basement of John A. Brown's Department Store. Four years later, after a developer built a suburban shopping mall farther south, they opened an upscale, Southern-style cafeteria in the new Reding Shopping Center, followed in 1960 with an even larger cafeteria in the Hillcrest Shopping Center at SW 59th Street and Pennsylvania Avenue.

Mobility and recreational eating also affected small towns. Marvin Jirous, born on a farm near Perry, opened the first drive-in in Fairview in 1958. It was a Dairy Boy. With little capital to invest, he leased a lot, ordered a sleek aluminum building from a company that offered financing, and made a deal with a dairy to delivery 90 gallons of ice cream mix every week. After stocking the drive-in, he had $14 left to make change on opening day. The menu was simple, with Coke, Dr Pepper, and ice cream cones for a nickel, fries for 15 cents, and hamburgers for a quarter. For six weeks Marvin and his wife Barbara ran the place, then hired two young women as employees. Two years later Jirous was recruited by Charlie Pappe to become the second franchisee of an embryonic chain of drive-ins called Sonic.

Naomi O'Mealy, a former cafeteria worker at Enid High School, started O'Mealy's Cafeterias
(OHS)

Beverly's Chicken in the Rough

Beverly Osborn, a native of Marlow, and his wife Rubye had been in the food business since 1921 with mixed success. In 1936, after closing several locations in the shadow of the Great Depression, they conceived a new restaurant that would cater to the traveling public and specialize in fried chicken served with shoestring potatoes and a biscuit. They called it "Chicken in the Rough." Their success included a memorable logo of a cigar-smoking rooster with a broken golf club and a new business model called franchising. By 1960 there were 234 Chicken in the Rough restaurants scattered along the nation's highways.

Beverly's Chicken in the Rough, Lincoln Boulevard, Oklahoma City, 1954 (OHS)

Beverly's
Chicken in
the Rough,
Oklahoma City, 1946
(OHS)

Service with the Speed of Sound

Although drive-in restaurants had been around for several decades by the 1950s, one Oklahoman developed a unique blend of ownership, management, efficiency, and food that would eventually create more wealth at the grassroots level than any other one business in Oklahoma history. That man was Troy Smith and his creative concept was Sonic.

Smith, the son of an oilfield worker, walked onto the stage of history after World War II with more ambition than money. He drove a truck, saved a little, and borrowed enough to buy a small café in Shawnee. By 1953 he had worked hard enough to open a white-tablecloth steak house that had a small root beer stand in front called Top Hat. Noticing that the drive-in generated higher net profit than the steak house, he hired car hops, built canopies to protect the car hops from the rain, installed speakers for music, and improvised an intercom system so customers could order from their car, which led to the slogan, "Service With the Speed of Sound." In 1959, reinforced by his new partner Charlie Pappe, Smith decided to franchise the concept.

The start-up company, called Sonic because the name Top Hat had already been trademarked, grew on a lean budget that relied on multiple owners, low overhead, and managers motivated by profit sharing. Typically, Troy and Charlie would select a town and site for a Sonic, find investors to build a small building that was simply a kitchen with canopies, and hire a manager who made a small salary with the promise of bonuses and dividends. To minimize investment needs, Troy and Charlie kept the franchise fee low, but collected two and a half cents for every hamburger sold. Further economy was gained when Troy signed a deal with Cardinal Paper Company to supply the hamburger sacks, track the number used, and collect the fees that were then passed to the central office.

To help expand the growing chain of drive-ins, Troy recruited Marvin Jirous from the Alva store to be president of Sonic Supply from 1967 to 1972 and president of Sonic from 1973 to 1980. It was a time of explosive growth as the chain became a regional phenomenon with more than 1,200 stores. Following hard times during the 1980s, the company retrenched but rebounded with new growth in the 1990s. Cliff Hudson, an attorney and community leader whose father had been a developer and builder in Oklahoma City, guided the company into a new era with the

core business plan intact but fortified with national advertising, consistent quality control, and technological innovations. By 2015 Sonic: America's Drive-in was a national brand with more than 3,500 stores coast to coast.

Marvin Jirous
(Marvin Jirous)

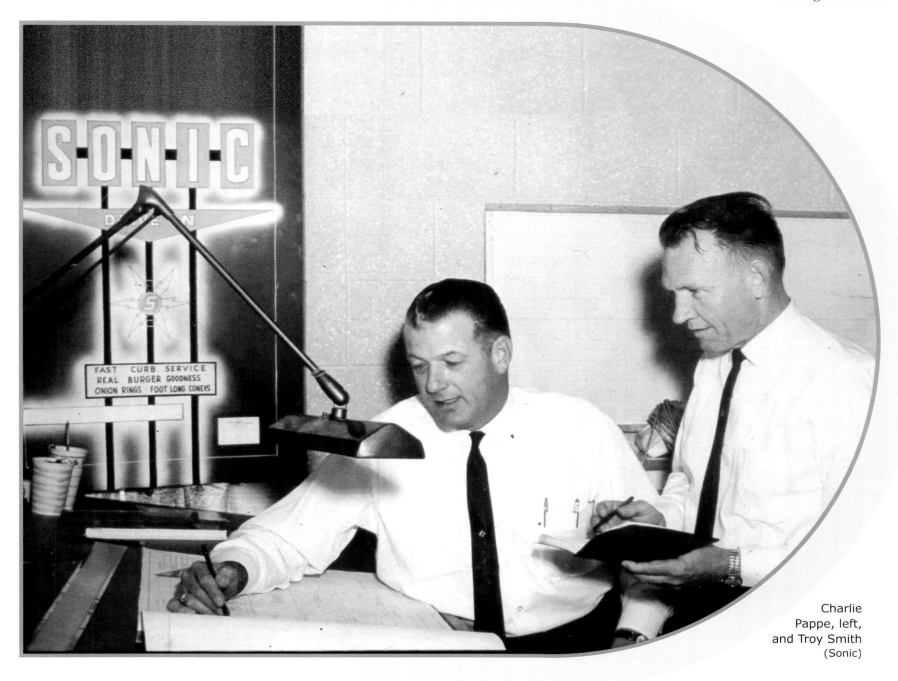

Charlie
Pappe, left,
and Troy Smith
(Sonic)

Pete Prichard, left, founder of Pete's Place, Krebs (OHS)

The World, One Plate at a Time

With more disposable income and the mobility to satisfy cravings for exotic flavors, Oklahomans developed a growing appetite for international food in the 1960s and 1970s. Investors willing to work long hours, usually first- or second-generation immigrants with the support of family members, supplied the variety.

Pepe's Mexican Restaurant, Edmond advertising $2.50 Wednesday Special (Julian Gonzalez Family)

Pete's Place

As a first generation Italian immigrant, Pete Prichard had few options when his leg was crushed in a coal mining accident in 1916. Hard labor was impossible, but he knew how to cook, he knew how to brew beer, and he liked people, so he started serving beer and food out of his home in Krebs. By 1925 he called it Pete's Place. As Pete's clientele grew, he expanded from the kitchen to partitioned bedrooms, then to additional rooms as needed. By World War II Pete's Place consisted of one sprawling home split into nine small dining rooms on the ground floor.

By 1960 Pete's Place in Krebs had a small but devoted following of patrons who drove long distances for unique Italian food that had been served in the old Prichard home since 1916. After the Indian Nations Turnpike and Lake Eufaula were completed, Pete's son, Billy Joe Prichard, decided to expand both the restaurant and the marketing. With Catherine, his wife and business manager, they added a new sign, pursued bus tours, and enclosed the covered front porch for a banquet room that could seat 100 diners. Those improvements were passed on to Pete's grandson, Joe, who had grown up in the restaurant and honed his skills with a restaurant management degree from OSU. With his wife and partner, Kathy, they added merchandise for another stream of revenue, created a new subsidiary to brew and distribute Choc Beer, and converted the old banquet space into private dining rooms reminiscent of the original Pete's Place. Their three children were still in the family business in 2015.

El Charrito

Luis Alvarado was another pioneer in international foods who expanded his business in the 1960s. He opened his first Mexican restaurant in 1937 at the corner of NW 10th Street and Dewey Avenue in Oklahoma City. When a fire destroyed that building he moved to the Paseo District and renamed his place El Charrito, translated as "Little Cowboy." By 1967 Alvarado was managing six locations in Oklahoma City when his brother-in-law suggested they merge their restaurants into one regional chain called El Chico. Meanwhile, Alvarado's son-in-law, Julian Gonzales, used some of the original family recipes to open Pepe's in Edmond and Laredo's in Oklahoma City. His son, Julian Gonzalez Jr., continued the family tradition and opened Casa de los Milagros on Classen Boulevard. In Spanish it meant "House of Miracles."

The original Pete's Place, Krebs
(Prichard Family)

(El Chico Restaurants)

Jamil's

In 1957, with interstate highways changing traffic and shopping patterns, Jim Jamil Elias moved his restaurant to 51st Street and Yale Avenue in Tulsa. Using family recipes brought from Lebanon to Oklahoma by his parents, Jamil's earned a reputation for the hummus, tabouli, cabbage rolls, pita bread, smoked bologna, and pork rib served with every steak dinner. In 1964 Jamil opened a second restaurant at a busy highway crossroads north of the State Capitol in Oklahoma City, and by the time of his death in 1979 he also operated restaurants in Houston and Dallas.

Triple XXX Root Beer "Thirst Station" serving customers, 1932 (OHS)

Triple AAA

In 1938 Doyle Carpenter worked with a pharmacist from Fairfax named Albert Rochau to develop a new formula for root beer. They opened their first drive-in restaurant at NW 13th Street and Broadway Avenue in Oklahoma City and called it Triple AAA Root Beer Thirst Station. The distinctive structure had been built by XXX Root Beer in the shape of a barrel. After expanding to several locations across five states, the business hit hard times in 1960 when the key ingredient, sassafras oil, was banned. In 2012, using a variation of the original recipe, Justin Thomas, owner of the Bricktown Candy Company, resurrected the brand, which he sold in Bricktown and at POPS in Arcadia.

Jamil's, Tulsa
(Tulsa Historical Society)

Early QuikTrip Convenience Store, Tulsa (QuikTrip)

Looking for Adventure

The pace of life accelerated for many people from the 1960s to the 1980s. In the public sector the demand for speed, convenience, and access was satisfied with programs such as interstate highways and deregulation of trucking. In the private sector that same demand was satisfied by businessmen and women who provided goods and services when, where, and how they could turn a profit.

Tom and Judy Love
(Love's)

Love's

Oklahoma City natives Tom and Judy Love opened their first gasoline service station in 1964 at the junction of two highways in Watonga. To minimize capital investment, Tom leased an outdated, empty service station, ordered a truckload of gasoline with 30 days to pay, and found a hard-working country boy willing to work for low wages with a commission based on sales. Over the next seven years, with the simple slogan "The Cheapest Gas in Town," Tom and Judy used cash flow to open more service stations in small towns while experimenting with a combination of longer hours, self-service gasoline, and a growing line of groceries found in traditional convenience stores. In 1971 the first Love's Country Store sign was installed in Guymon. When Tom's successful business model was challenged again in the 1970s, he and his team responded with a super-sized Country Store located on the interstate highway system. They called it a Love's Travel Stop. By 2015, after branching into fuel trading and transport, the system of Love's Country Stores and Travel Stops had reached more than 300 locations coast to coast.

Love's Travel Stops & Country Stores Holcomb, Kansas (Love's)

QuikTrip

Chester Cadieux
(Tulsa Historical Society)

A similar shift in an original business model, although in reverse order, made a local convenience store a regional brand with headquarters in Tulsa. The company was QuikTrip and the innovator was Chester Cadieux, a native of Tulsa who invested $5,000 to join Burt Holmes and a couple of other investors to open their first store in 1958. By 1971 they had grown the chain to 57 convenience stores when Cadieux and his leadership team decided to add gasoline sales. That made a huge difference, along with other innovations such as 24-hour operations, profit sharing for employees, an unconditional guarantee of gasoline quality, and a catchy television ad campaign featuring Lamar and the Cowboy. By 2015, led by Chet Cadieux as president, the QuikTrip system had more than 725 stores in 11 states and employed more than 20,000 people.

Chet Cadieux
(*Tulsa World*)

Oklahoma
Route 66 West
(ODOT)

Route 66 Motel,
Barstow, CA
(Shellee Graham)

The Mother Road

A contrasting reaction to the accelerating pace of life in the 1960s and 1970s was the growing allure of two-lane roads and lost Americana. Reinforced by the fruits of historic preservation at both the national and local levels, a new business sector emerged that banked on the public's attraction to neon signs, forgotten motor courts, and roadside attractions. There was no better place to find those treasures than on Route 66, the Mother Road.

Lucille's

Soon after work on Route 66 started in 1925, tourists needing gasoline and a peaceful night's rest created a market for new investment. One of the earliest waystations in Oklahoma was a two-story stucco structure built in 1929 a few miles east of Weatherford. The most famous owner was Lucille Hamons, who lived on the second floor, operated the service station on the ground floor, and managed the adjacent motor court. Now known as Lucille's, the quaint building still stands alongside a long stretch of the original roadbed, visible from Interstate 40.

Lucille's
Route 66 West
(ODOT)

Foyil Totem Pole Park

In 1937, two years before John Steinbeck would make Route 66 a household name in *The Grapes of Wrath*, a manual arts teacher retired from an orphanage in Sand Springs and invested his time and money in what would become one of the most famous folk art attractions on the Mother Road. The creative genius was Ed Galloway and his creation was the Foyil Totem Pole Park, located northeast of Claremore. The first feature completed was the central totem pole, a 90-foot-tall piece of painted concrete resting on the back of a turtle with 200 images of American Indians, symbols, and animal figures. Another feature of the park was the Fiddle House, an 11-sided structure where Galloway built and sold fiddles to passing tourists. In 2015 the park was maintained by the Rogers County Historical Society and the Foyil Heritage Association.

Ed Galloway's 90 foot Totem Pole on Oklahoma State Highway 28A, 3.5 miles east of U.S. Route 66, Foyil
(National Park Service)

Big
Blue
Whale,
Catoosa
(Library of Congress)

The Blue Whale

In the early 1970s, as the Mother Road was losing traffic to toll roads and interstate highways, Hugh Davis built a blue whale next to a spring-fed pond near the little town of Catoosa. Originally it was intended to be an anniversary gift for his wife, who collected whale figurines, but it quickly became a landmark with commercial value. Davis added picnic tables, sand beaches, and a replica of Noah's ark. Across the street he opened the Indian Trading Post where his brother-in-law made pipes and other tourist souvenirs. Community groups have since restored the iconic Blue Whale.

POPS

In 2007, with the international popularity of Route 66 still gaining momentum, Oklahoma oilman and entrepreneur Aubrey McClendon opened a new iconic attraction on the Mother Road near Arcadia. He called it POPS. Designed by award-winning architect Rand Elliott, the ultra-modern gas station, restaurant, gift shop, and event venue featured architectural elements such as a 110-foot cantilevered canopy and a 66-foot-tall sculptural pop bottle illuminated by LED lights. Inside, the road theme continued with souvenirs and more than 600 different soda pop varieties for sale, including more than 80 root beers. As Oklahoma natives McClendon and Elliott proved, the substance and spirit of Route 66 is still alive.

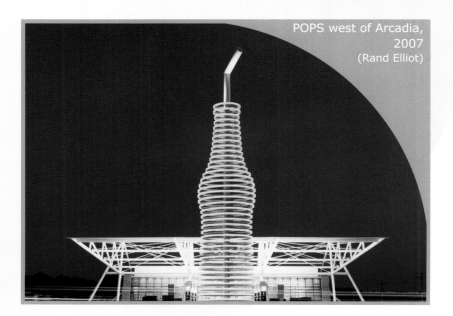

POPS west of Arcadia, 2007 (Rand Elliot)

Mercy Hospital and School of Nursing, Oklahoma City (OHS)

Frontiers of Health Care

By 1960 the world of health care was on the threshold of new frontiers that combined healing, science, and commerce. Greater access to health insurance, combined with congressional passage of Medicare in 1965, accelerated the changes as businessmen and women responded with new clinics, bigger hospitals, and innovative treatments.

John and Eleanor Kirkpatrick
(Kirkpatrick Family Archives)

Secrets of the Heart

The foundation of health care in Oklahoma had been laid by nonprofit hospitals and business people willing to invest in medicine and research. William K. Warren, who had once owned the world's largest fleet of oil railroad tank cars, created a foundation in Tulsa and dedicated his life's work to St. Francis Hospital, opened in 1960 at a cost of $7.5 million.

Another philanthropist with a heart was John Kirkpatrick, a native of Oklahoma City who made a fortune in oil and banking after World War II. In 1956 John and his wife Eleanor made three investments that would open new doors of opportunity in health care. They helped organize the Frontiers of Science Foundation and the Medical Research Foundation. Both were community-based efforts dedicated to merging science and healing. That same year John joined the board of Mercy Hospital, created in 1947 and led by the dynamic director of the nursing college, Sister Mary Coletta. The Kirkpatricks, joined by the Sisters of Mercy, would embrace a young man destined to change the world of health care. His name was Dr. Nazih Zuhdi.

St. Francis Hospital, Tulsa (OHS)

Exploring New Frontiers

A native of Lebanon, Dr. Zuhdi had a prestigious medical degree from the American University in Beirut and five years working with the first generation of pioneers in the field of open-heart surgery. Those formative years with colleagues such as Dr. Clarence Dennis and Dr. C. Walter Lillehei taught him the surgical healing powers necessary to preserve life and inspired him to conquer the Mount Everest of medical science—a procedure that would allow a heart-lung machine to maintain basic functions of life while surgeons repaired the heart.

Despite incremental progress in design and function, the fundamental problem remained how to get oxygen into the bloodsteam without creating microscopic bubbles that could kill a patient. The pursuit of this solution was foremost in his mind in 1957 when Dr. Zuhdi accepted an invitation to start an open heart surgery program at the University of Oklahoma. By the time he arrived in Oklahoma, Dr. Zuhdi had the skill sets, training, and self-confidence needed in the risk-taking world of medical research.

Caption in the *Oklahoma Times,* March 29, 1985, "Nancy Rogers, the first person to receive a heart transplant in Oklahoma, leans on her physician, Dr. Nazih Zuhdi, at a press conference Friday." (OHS)

Charting His Own Path

When Dr. Zuhdi's relentless pursuit of new science quickly outgrew the mission of a university teaching hospital, the Sisters of Mercy and John Kirkpatrick stepped up to open a new path for exploration. They invited Dr. Zuhdi and two of his colleagues to join the staff at Mercy Hospital. Then the oilman turned philanthropist offered to build a state-of-the-art laboratory in an old operating room on the fourth floor of the hospital. While all of this was unfolding, Dr. Zuhdi performed the first open heart surgery in Oklahoma on January 8, 1959.

Zuhdi's first discovery in the laboratory was a method to slow the flow rate of blood through internal hypothermia. He created a double helix, a stainless steel tube inside a plastic tube, to cool the blood so surgeons had more time to operate. The second discovery was total intentional hemodilution, a revolutionary process that used a solution of 5 percent dextrose in water instead of blood as a priming fluid in the heart-lung machine. Through repeated testing on animals, he documented that these innovations improved circulation, tissue metabolism, and postoperative progress.

On February 25, 1960, Dr. Zuhdi used the double helix and total intentional hemodilution for the first time during open heart surgery with a patient, Gene Nix. The revolutionary impact was best summarized by Dr. Dwight Harkem at the University of Minnesota. "Nazih's discovery popularized open heart surgery and made it universal so it could be done like any other surgery. He made it accessible to all." Scientists and physicians from around the world beat a path to Oklahoma to learn the secrets of Dr. Zuhdi's revolutionary procedures.

Dr. Nazih Zuhdi
(OHS)

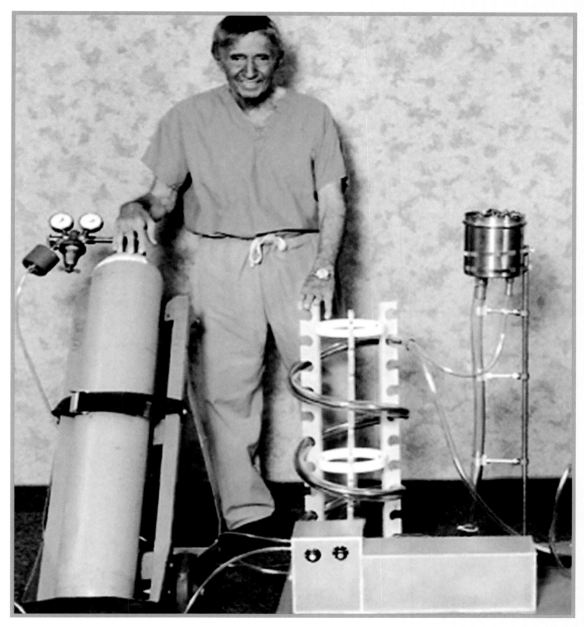

Dr. Nazih Zuhdi poses
with the total intentional
hemodilution equipment
(OHS)

In 1984 Dr. Zuhdi joined the staff at Integris Baptist Medical Center, where he continued his research and founded the Oklahoma Transplant Institute, later renamed in his honor. A year after founding the Oklahoma Transplant Institute, on March 3, 1985, Dr. Zuhdi and his colleagues performed the first successful heart transplant in Oklahoma. His patient was Nancy Rogers.

Don Hodges,
KOMA disc jockey
(OHS)

The Voice of Mass Communication

From 1960 to 1982 the broadcast industry matured as a multilayered source of information, entertainment, and music. Whether it was radio, television, or the recording industry, the new giants of mass communication drove the economy as an avenue for investment that reached thousands of potential customers through advertising and sales.

Bill Howard, right, with Jude Northcutt
on *the Jude 'n' Jody Show*,
Oklahoma City
(Howard Family)

The Sounds of Commerce

Since 1921 most radio stations had offered a predictable mixture of live music, drama, news, and feeds from networks such as CBS and NBC. All of this changed in the 1960s and 1970s. First, television provided fierce competition, while the recording industry supplied a steady stream of music that filled air time at little cost. The next big change was talk radio, which emerged with raw energy.

KOMA began broadcasting in 1922 with 15 watts of power. From the 1930s to the 1950s, with studios filling the 24th floor of the Biltmore Hotel in Oklahoma City, the power increased but the programming remained tame. All of that changed in 1958 when Todd Storz bought the station and introduced a Top 40 format filled with the new sounds of rock and roll. With 50,000 watts of power at 1520 on the AM dial, KOMA could be heard across the American West every night. Linda Ronstadt, growing up in Arizona, would later cite KOMA as her first exposure to rock and roll. Throughout the 1960s and 1970s, KOMA featured a magical blend

KRMG host, John Erling (KRMG)

of disc jockey personality, contests, fun, and great music. Ty and Tony Tyler, sons of radio pioneer Ralph Tyler, purchased KOMA and a cluster of other stations for $40 million in 2012.

Robert S. Kerr and Dean McGee, who had created the oil company Kerr-McGee ten years earlier, invested in a new Tulsa radio station in 1949. They called it KRMG. In 1976, after the station had converted to an adult contemporary music format, managers hired a young disc jockey who had been in radio since 1961. His name was John Erling. When talk radio swept the nation in the early 1980s, he made a seamless transition to the new format with humor, satire, and fun controversy. One long-running gag was his promotion of the Tulsa Mountains, what he called "theater of the mind" where "a headlong slalom down exciting Pantyhose Run can be accomplished without a snag." In 2015 Erling was producing an acclaimed series of web-based oral histories in association with the University of Tulsa.

Towers of Power

Not since the invention of moveable type and the dawn of newspapers had there been a similar revolution in mass communication. The transformative new technology was television.

E. K. Gaylord had been in the newspaper business since 1903 and the owner of a radio station since 1928 when he paid $5,000 for WKY. In 1936 he said he soon would bring to Oklahoma a new technology called television, a feat he accomplished in 1939 with an experimental broadcast staged by NBC engineers in the Municipal Auditorium in Oklahoma City. Delayed by the war, Gaylord secured the first federal license for a television station in Oklahoma and went on the air with WKY-TV on June 6, 1949. That first day of broadcasting started with a welcome from Governor Roy Turner and Gaylord, a film about D-Day, a children's show called *Gizmo Goodkins*, a talk show, and music by Wiley and Gene followed by Ken Wright on the Kilgen Organ. The day ended with a Hopalong Cassidy film. Two years later Gaylord built a new station and broadcast tower at a high spot on N. Britton Road. In December of 1951 WKY-TV showed its first monthly profit of $18.64. Years later, ownership and the call letters would change to KFOR.

A similar investment strategy in broadcast stations was followed by the Griffin family of Muskogee. John T. Griffin, who had created the Griffin Grocery Company in 1908, was fascinated by radio technology. He founded KTUL-Radio in Tulsa in the early 1930s and followed by purchasing KOMA-Radio in Oklahoma City in 1938. After World War II he started researching opportunities in television, a quest that

was accomplished by his son John and son-in-law Jimmy Leake, who purchased licenses for stations KTVX in Muskogee (soon with new call letters KTUL-TV in Tulsa) and KWTV in Oklahoma City. In April of 1954 John earned international attention when he completed a 1,572-foot antenna tower for KWTV that was declared the world's tallest man-made structure. The top 10-foot portion of that tower, taken down in 2015, is on display at the Oklahoma History Center. David Griffin, grandson of John T., became president of Griffin Broadcasting in 1990, purchased KOTV in Tulsa, and in 2000 entered a joint venture with the Oklahoma Publishing Company to start a groundbreaking web-based news service called NewsOK.com.

KWTV tower, Oklahoma City (OHS)

The WKY Kilgen Organ

E. K. Gaylord, pioneer newspaper publisher and convert to the potential of radio, expressed his faith in the future in 1936 when he spent $33,000 to buy a new four-manual, 14-rank theater-style pipe organ manufactured by the Kilgen Organ Company. A week after the organ was installed in his Skirvin Tower WKY studios, it was played by a new staff musician named Ken Wright. Wright would be associated with the Kilgen for the rest of his life.

In 1949 the Kilgen was moved to the new WKY-TV studio in the Municipal Auditorium, where it was played by Wright on the first broadcast. Two years later, Gaylord sold the Kilgen to the Oklahoma City Symphony Orchestra. Conductor Guy Frasier Harrison played the organ, as did a number of guest artists. After the Kilgen was reconditioned in 1977, it was used irregularly until

Ken Wright at the organ (OHS)

Kilgen Organ and the WKY band, 1939 (OHS)

1998, when it was removed from the soon-to-be restored Civic Center Music Hall and stored until a new home could be found. With the urging of local businessman Greg Robertson, that new home was the Oklahoma History Center.

The driving force behind the restoration of the Kilgen was business pioneer and inventor Garman Kimmell, who along with his company and family, donated the funds to bring the instrument back to life. In 2017, with the help of Kimmell's son-in-law Dusty Miller and the staff at the American Organ Institute, a division of the School of Music at the University of Oklahoma, the mighty Kilgen will once again will be played in its full glory in the Devon Great Hall of the Oklahoma History Center.

Kilgen
pipe organ
in the Skirvin
Tower, 1936
(OHS)

A carving of the Greek
god Pan at the WKY studio
(OHS)

Commercial Break

Television provided a powerful new means of delivering a sales pitch to potential customers in the comfort of their living rooms. Using all the arts of communication, commercials were illustrated short stories offering reasons why customers should buy a particular service or product. The creativity in attracting an audience to those messages was boundless.

Foreman Scotty on the set of the Circle 4 Ranch (OHS)

3D Danny promoting Shredded Wheat Juniors, c. 1950 (OHS)

First National Bank of Oklahoma City

In 1969, when this commercial was produced, the First National Bank of Oklahoma City was the largest and most entrepreneurial bank in the region. Led by Charles Vose, Sr., the bank could trace its heritage back to the land run of 1889 and a merger in 1930 that led to the construction of the tallest building in Oklahoma City prior to the Devon Tower.

Coca-Cola and Anita Bryant

In the early 1960s Oklahoma-born and raised recording artist Anita Bryant became the national spokesperson for Coca Cola. Her career paralleled the rise of television as a tool for marketing, starting with her appearances on WKY in 1949 and a show she hosted as a teenager. In addition to her Coca Cola commercials on national networks, she was the featured halftime entertainment at two televised Super Bowls and became the national spokesperson for Florida Orange Juice in a series of commercials. Her career continues to the present time as part of her Anita Bryant Ministries.

QuikTrip

In 1958 Burt Holmes and Chester Cadieux opened their first QuikTrip in Tulsa. In 2015 there are more than 700 stores in eleven states.

B. C. Clark

In 1929 B. C. Clark opened his jewelry store in downtown Oklahoma City. In 1956 the company created the familiar B. C. Clark jingle that is still used.

Doenges Ford

In 1968 Bill and Bob Doenges acquired the downtown Tulsa Ford dealership from their father. In 1974 the brothers started another dealership in a more suburban location in Tulsa.

BancFirst

Since 2005 BancFirst and the Ackerman-McQueen advertising agency have produced more than 20 television commercials based on the themes of local pride and loyalty to customers. The roots of Bancfirst go back to 1966 when Gene Rainbolt purchased a bank in Shawnee. In 1989 he consolidated multiple banks into one state charter and adopted the name Bancfirst. His son, David Rainbolt, became chief executive officer in 1992 and sought the services of Ackerman-McQueen to create a new brand. Jeanette Elliot, creative services director, and her team developed a unique style of images and narrative that emphasized the local leadership of each bank and their commitment to a sense of community.

Use the QR code reader app on your mobile device to see and hear the commercials.

Eskimo Joes

By 1987 Stan Clark had established his highly successful Eskimo Joe's restaurant in Stillwater, Oklahoma, and he had created a successful line of clothing depicting his famous logo.

Ozarka

The Oklahoma City Ozarka Water Company was founded in 1907. The current owners, the Raupe family, purchased the business in 1971. Russell Westbrook starred in one commercial.

Kerr-McGee

In 1946 Robert S. Kerr and Dean McGee founded Kerr-McGee Oil Industries and sold gasoline and oil under the brands of Tulsa-based Deep Rock and Enid-based Knox. Kerr-McGee eventually opened service stations under the corporate name with a line of oil and gas products.

Mathis Brothers

By 1960 Don and Bud Mathis' furniture store and their country music variety show created a very successful business model in Oklahoma City. In 2015 there are nearly twenty Mathis Brothers Furniture stores in Oklahoma and California.

Soundtrak

The electronic stores named Soundtrack lasted from 1975 to 1993. Co-owner Linda Verin took on the Linda Soundtrak persona to advertise the Oklahoma franchise.

Braum's

In 1968 Braum's opened its first Oklahoma store in Oklahoma City. In 2015 the company had 275 stores in five states.

TG&Y

In the 1930s three small-town merchants in western Oklahoma combined their purchasing power to create a central warehouse that would reduce costs and give them a competitive advantage against other variety stores. They used the first letters of their last names to come up with TG&Y.

Use the QR code reader app on your mobile device to see and hear the commercials.

BancFirst
Claremore
commercial
(BancFirst)

Live and On the Air

The ability to connect sponsors with potential customers relied on the popularity and demographics of a particular show, whether it was a newscast appealing to adults or an adventure show for children. From the 1950s to the 1960s, a combination of local talent, willing sponsors, and baby boomers hooked on television opened the door to an amazing era of creativity live and on the air.

Danny Williams started and ended his career on radio, but for a generation of kids in central Oklahoma, he was Dan D Dynamo, superintendent of the Space Science Center, friend of Bazark the Robot, and master of futuristic machines such as the synchro-retroverter, physco-peerscope, and physi-tempometer. Beating the *Mickey Mouse Club* in the 4 p.m. time slot, Danny operated out of Arcrod City, his home planet, and worked with his allies the Mescians who could neither be seen nor heard without special ear plugs. Danny would have other roles on television, such as host of *Saturday Night Wrestling* ("Watch

Miss Ida on *Romper Room* (OHS)

out for flying chairs!") and *Danny's Day*, but to a generation of Oklahomans, he was 3D Danny.

Another must-see children's show was *Foreman Scotty*, "live from the Circle 4 Ranch." The talent behind the cowboy character was Steve Powell, who developed his first show *Deputy Chris* in Tulsa before moving to Oklahoma City in 1955. Features of the show included interviews with kids, Woody the Birthday Horse, and the adventures of Foreman Scotty and his friends, including Xavier T. Willard (Danny Williams) and Cannonball McCoy (Wilson Hurst). One lucky kid got the golden horseshoe when the magic lasso landed on him or her. Of course, everyone first had to shout the magic word, "Nix-O-Billy."

In 1958, three months after KOCO-TV opened studios in an old grocery store on Britton Road, a young school teacher named Ida Blackburn went on the air as Miss Ida in the syndicated educational show *Romper Room*. For $60 a week, Miss Ida taught lessons to four preschoolers five days a week,

Ho Ho
the Clown, right
(Howard Family)

including the ways of "do bee" and "don't bee." With only one camera on the studio set, she would turn away from the kids and narrate commercials for local companies such as Borden's Milk and Dennis Doughnuts. Blackburn would go on in her career to host a long-running magazine format show as Ida B.

Ho Ho the Clown, Ed Birchall in real life, joined the lineup at KOCO in 1959 with a Saturday morning cartoon show. Four years later he moved to the coveted noontime slot Monday to Friday, going up against the news on the other two channels. With his trick dog Jeannie and sharp-witted sidekick Pokey the Puppet, played to perfection by stage manager-turned-comic Bill Howard, Ho Ho blended cartoons and short films with comedy skits and educational lessons.

Leon Russell arranging at Gold Star Studio in Los Angeles, c. 1965 (OHS)

Home Sweet Oklahoma

For a few years in the early 1970s, music and magic merged in an abandoned church in Tulsa. Today, we think of the music made in the soundproofed rooms of that special place, but in 1972 it was a major investment that required a leap of faith and a willingness to take a risk.

Leon Russell, whose family name was Russell Bridges, was born in Lawton but raised in Tulsa. At the age of 19, armed with ambition and talent, he moved to Los Angeles where he earned a reputation as a gifted studio musician, arranger, and singer-songwriter. By 1972, following his breakout solo debut and a starring role in the rock and roll movie "Mad Dogs and Englishmen" with Joe Cocker, he was one of the top grossing musical acts in the world.

With fame and money, Leon the entrepreneur came home and invested in three Oklahoma studios. One was in his house in Tulsa. Another was in his house on Grand Lake. The third and most famous was in an abandoned Church of God building at Third Street and Trenton Avenue near downtown Tulsa. Leon and his partner, British producer Denny Cordell, called it the Shelter Church Studio.

Leon's studios were filled with the best equipment available. At a time when high-end tape recorders cost $1,000 per track, Leon commissioned the world's first 40-track machine from John Stephens. Only seven such decks were ever built, and Leon had two of them as he pushed the limits of creativity. Other equipment included Ampex and 3M tape machines and some of the world's best recording consoles. Along with the best equipment came some of the best sound engineers such as J J Cale, an Oklahoma singer-songwriter who preferred life at the console mixing music.

Sweet Emily, left, and Leon Russell in Tulsa, 1970 (OHS)

Church Studio, Tulsa
(OHS)

Tulsa Magic

The Church, coupled with Leon's studios at this home and on the lake, attracted some of the most talented artists in the world who wanted to either record a song or just hang out with Leon and his friends. Eric Clapton and George Harrison came often. Bob Dylan made a visit to the lake house. Tom Petty recorded his first album with Leon and crew at the controls. Other friends and patrons included Freddie King, Billy Preston, Peter Tosh, and J J Cale.

In 1979, after moving his studios to Los Angeles, Leon hired a young singer-songwriter and sound engineer from Oklahoma. His name was Steve Ripley. Ripley worked shoulder-to-shoulder with Leon and Cale at Leon's Paradise Studios, followed by a year in the studio and on the road playing guitar with Bob Dylan before he moved back to his native Oklahoma. In 1987, 10 years after Leon left Tulsa the second time, Ripley and partners bought the Church Studio and put it back in business. Magically, his first client was Leon Russell. When Ripley told Leon he was walking in his footsteps, Leon replied, "Steve, be careful where you step."

J J Cale at the
Whisky a Go-Go,
c. 1960
(OHS)

Smokaroma, Inc.,
President Maurice
Lee Jr., center
(OHS)

Chapter Six

Embracing Diversity

Made in Oklahoma is a symbol of the state's creative ability to connect supply and demand. Another symbol is tribal enterprise, a blend of deep roots in the entrepreneurial spirit of the West and tribal communities working together to achieve the greatest good for the greatest number of people. Still another symbol is the story of a city reinventing itself through a combination of community investment and private enterprise.

All six sections of this book, from 1716 to the present day, feature products and services made at the crossroads of commerce called Oklahoma. The diversity, from oil field equipment and helicopter parts to history books and barbeque sauce, reflects the willingness of Oklahoma businessmen and women to invest their time and resources to drive the wheels of economic development.

Artist rendering of the Oklahoma City Bricktown Canal
(Frankfurt-Short-Bruza)

The Power of Partnerships

Oklahoma's economy has always been a balancing act. At the fundamental level, the free enterprise system depends on supply and demand, producers and consumers, investors and workers. Another critical balancing act has been the partnership between public and private investment. There is no better single example of this balancing act than MAPS and the phoenix-like renaissance of downtown Oklahoma City.

Mayor Ron Norick, 1995
(OHS)

The Miracle of MAPS

In 1993 Oklahoma City's economy was stuck in what some people have called the Second Great Depression, a gloomy time that began with the collapse of the deep gas drilling boom, deepened with bank failures, and hardened with a toxic real estate sector. Shock therapy was needed to regain a sense of balance.

Leading the way out of this morass was Ron Norick, a third-generation president of a successful printing enterprise who was elected mayor of Oklahoma City in 1988. His first attempt to jump start the economy mirrored past efforts to attract outsiders to save the city with instant investments and jobs. When incentives to lure an airlines maintenance center failed, Norick and the business community realized the people of Oklahoma City first had to help themselves as a community, which hopefully would stimulate private investment. The result of their planning effort was called Metropolitan Area Projects, MAPS for short.

The concept was a cash-driven, five-year penny sales tax to be invested in nine projects, all downtown with the exception of new horse barns at the State Fairgrounds. The list included improvements to the Civic Center Music Hall and the Convention Center; a new library, baseball stadium, and nearby sports arena; improvements to the riverfront and public transportation; and the construction of a boat canal that would connect the riverfront and central business district with an old industrial zone-turned-entertainment-venue called Bricktown. On December 14, 1993, the people of Oklahoma City approved the investment of a penny sales tax. As work on the projects progressed, the energy and real estate sectors started a slow recovery, that combined with new community incentives for historic preservation to stimulate even more investment and a sense that good times were around the corner. As Norick and his fellow leaders had predicted, MAPS was a bridge to a brighter future.

Architectural rendering of the MAPS $80 million sports arena, 1996
(Frankfurt-Short-Bruza Collection)

Big League City

While the citizens of Oklahoma City invested in infrastructure through MAPS, businessmen and women with the necessary skill sets, assets, and willingness to take a risk were climbing out of the economic doldrums that had reached bottom in the 1990s. At the time, no one could have dreamed that the state would soon have its own NBA team.

The steps leading to that historic convergence of opportunity and action can best be traced through the experience of Clay Bennett. Born and raised in Oklahoma, Bennett was well prepared as an entrepreneur, community leader, and sports executive. He had served as executive director of the Olympic Sports Festival in 1989 and was on the management team that owned and operated the Oklahoma Redhawks baseball team. Most importantly, he had served on the board of directors of the San Antonio Spurs, where he learned about the business side of a major league sports franchise and worked with David Stern, commissioner of the NBA.

In 2005, a day after Hurricane Katrina devastated much of New Orleans, Stern called Bennett and made an offer. If he and the business community would work with city leaders to craft a sustainable business plan, the New Orleans Hornets basketball team would relocate to Oklahoma City and play 35 games during the season. With the new MAPS arena available and solid support from city and state officials, Bennett and his associates accepted the risk. The Hornets played two seasons in Oklahoma before returning to New Orleans. As Bennett would later recall, "it was a real time test that Oklahoma could support an NBA team."

Clay Bennett, right, with former NBA Commissioner David Stern (Clayton Bennett)

165

Thunder Up

Convinced that an NBA team was a good investment, Bennett and his associates offered to buy an interest in the Hornets before the end of the second season. The owner declined the offer but confirmed that Oklahoma could support a team. The search widened.

Joining Bennett in pursuit of a franchise were pillars of the business community. Aubrey McClendon and Tom Ward had built ground-breaking businesses in the energy industry. Jeff Records was a third-generation banker with a knack for entrepreneurial ventures. Bob Howard had expanded from car dealerships to real estate development. Jay Scaramucci, president of a privately held manufacturing company, was an active investor. Bill Cameron was president of a nationally recognized insurance company. And Everett Dobson, a native of Elk City, had helped usher in the dawn of the cellular telephone

Rumble the Bison, mascot of the Oklahoma City Thunder (OKC Thunder)

revolution. Willing to take a risk, these investors found their opportunity in 2006 when they bought the Seattle SuperSonics for $350 million. On April 18, 2008, NBA owners approved moving the franchise from Seattle to Oklahoma City. Soon, Oklahoma had a team called the Thunder.

The impact of the Thunder took two tracks. One was image. Within the borders of the state, the Thunder created a sense of unity and pride that would have long-lasting results, while outside the state, the Thunder and its prominence on national television put Oklahoma on the map as a good place to live, work, and play. The other impact was economic, including direct spending per game, player and staff salaries, and sales for food and recreation. The economic windfall, combined with the impact on Oklahoma's image, is testimony to the power of partnerships.

Oklahoma City Thunder
(OKC Thunder)

Build It and They Will Come

By 2005 the impact of public investment through MAPS was merging with the recovery of energy and real estate to create new opportunities for private investors willing to take a risk. Faint signs of improvement could be seen in all directions, with plans for a boat house on the river, the Hornets basketball team playing in the MAPS-funded arena, and new businesses popping up along Auto Alley and in Midtown.

One investor who saw an opportunity on this fast-changing stage of history was Avis Scaramucci, a native of Altus and a University of Oklahoma music major who had built a successful gift shop, bakery, and restaurant in the suburbs of Oklahoma City. In 2005, with Bricktown still more brick than town, she decided to take a leap and relocate to an old brick building across the street from the baseball park. "It was a gamble to build a fine dining restaurant and retail gift shop downtown," she said, "but I wanted to be in the middle of the

community. I'm in the people business." The new attraction was called Nona's, featuring fine dining, fresh vegetables grown in her own greenhouses, baked goods, and gifts. Nona's would set the standard for other businesses soon coming to Bricktown.

In 2004 Chip Fudge was ready for a new challenge. The entrepreneur had guided his company through a growth phase, and he had already bought a couple of historic buildings along Classen Boulevard when Oklahoma designer David Wanzer shared research about a distinctive but troubled district on the western fringe of downtown Oklahoma City. He called it Film Row, but most people called it Skid Row. Fudge, like Wanzer, saw through the debris of time. He bought one building, then another, and started using recently enacted state tax credits for historic rehabilitation to bring them back to life. To draw people, support the arts, and create buzz about a cool new neighborhood, he practically donated space to several organizations such as public radio station KOSU and Independent Artists of Oklahoma. By the time he launched a plan to move his company into the renovated Hart Building, the district was seen as a new hot spot in the inner city. As reporter Steve Lackmeyer observed, "Film Row shows that no area is beyond redemption." Once again, it was the power of partnerships.

Film Row, Oklahoma City
(David Waldo)

Sky Changer

In 2008 Devon Energy was a successful Oklahoma-based company that needed more and better office space. The question was where to build.

One option was to move to cheaper land in the suburbs. The other was to stay downtown and keep employees under one roof. Larry Nichols, co-founder, chairman of the board, and former CEO, decided to stay downtown for several reasons. Like Dean McGee, an urban pioneer of a previous generation, Nichols wanted to give back to the community and connect with the heartbeat of a city reborn after MAPS. The 50-story tower and surrounding complex included a five-story atrium accessible to the public, a public-private partnership to invest future tax revenue in surrounding neighborhoods, and an award-winning new design for the Myriad Gardens. As Nichols intended, the investment was a sky changer.

Devon Tower
(Devon Energy Corporation)

President Nixon signing the Indian Self-Determination and Education Assistance Act of 1975 (Nixon Foundation)

Tribal Enterprise

After the founding of the American Republic, national and state policy on Indian affairs followed a familiar script. Trade with the Indians when profitable, take their lands when needed, move them to reservations when convenient, and assimilate them into the mainstream of American life when possible. This assault on tribal sovereignty and culture started changing in the 1930s and took form in 1975 with self-governance and self-determination under federal law. Once that battle was won, tribal leaders in Oklahoma asked the next question. Without a large land base for taxation, how could they generate revenue to provide services to their people? The answer was tribal enterprise.

Senator Enoch Kelly Haney
(OHS)

Self Determination

Fortunately for Oklahoma tribes, free enterprise had been part of their culture for centuries, especially among the Cherokees, Choctaws, Chickasaws, and Creeks. In Tahlequah, Durant, Ada, Okmulgee, and other communities, the challenge was adapting those traditions to democratically elected governments that were just getting started with new constitutions.

W. W. Keeler, who would be the first elected principal chief of the Cherokees since statehood, also happened to be chief executive officer of Phillips Petroleum Company. Not willing to wait for a new constitution, he launched his tribe's first venture in 1969 and incorporated Cherokee Industries in Stillwell. By 2012 Cherokee Industries had progressed enough in capability and staffing to secure a contract with Walmart to evaluate and repackage 135,000 television sets a year. Two years later Cherokee Industries followed with a $2.5 million contract to produce frame assemblies and instrument panels for Sikorsky Helicopters. In 2015 the Cherokee Nation employed more than 3,000 people in tribal government and another 6,000 through Cherokee businesses.

The Chickasaw's first tribal enterprise was a motel in Sulphur bought out of bankruptcy and renovated with a grant. From the first day of operation, the venture employed 15 people and generated a positive cash flow for additional investments. Other ventures followed, such as gaming centers, banks, clinics, farms, Bedre Chocolates, and a world-class hotel and convention center called The Artesian. In 2015 the Chickasaws managed 60 separate businesses with more than 13,000 employees and a payroll exceeding $1.5 billion. Bill Lance, chief executive officer of Chickasaw Enterprises, summarized the impact. "The key takeaway for me," he said, "is the degree to which reinvestments in Oklahoma are paying dividends, particularly in how they continue to produce good jobs in rural Oklahoma…We consider the State of Oklahoma a partner, and we share a common goal to strengthen the economy and produce as many jobs as we can."

Left to right: Choctaw Chief Hollis Roberts, Oklahoma Governor David Walters, Cherokee Principal Chief Wilma Mankiller, and Chickasaw Governor Bill Anoatubby signing a compact, 1992. (OHS)

The Bottom Line

If tribal leaders have had a bottom line for their enterprises, it is the total value of services provided to tribal members mixed with benefits for the community at large. Those services have ranged from health care, housing, and educational opportunities to care for the elderly, language retention, and cultural preservation.

The Cherokees have taken the lead in using earned revenues for education. Since 2002 the tribe has given grants to school districts in the 14 counties of the old Cherokee Nation, including that part of Tulsa County in the Creek Nation. In 2014, with no strings attached, the affected school districts received more than $4 million from the Cherokee Nation. As the only tribe with its own syllabary, the Cherokees also have invested in language retention that includes emersion classes for youth, one-on-one tutorials for adults, and contracts with Google, Apple, and Microsoft to recognize Sequoyah's syllabary. In 2015 the tribe released the *New Testament* in the Cherokee language.

For more than 30 years, while reinvesting in growth industries and delivering services to tribal members, the Chickasaws have led the way in cultural preservation. It started with the Chickasaw Council House, a partnership with the Oklahoma Historical Society, and expanded to the Capitol Museum, the White House of the Chickasaws, and a $45 million investment in the award-winning Chickasaw Cultural Center near Sulphur. A special investment dear to Governor Bill Anoatubby was the Chickasaw Nation's Living Elders Project, which combined 48 oral histories and paintings by Chickasaw tribal member Mike Larsen to create a unique collection honoring elders. Those paintings represent a crossroads of commerce where the success of one business, the Chickasaw Nation, intersected with the skills sets of one businessman, Mike Larsen, to add value to the bottom line.

Cherokee Industries worker, 1981 (OHS)

Lessons Learned

The stories included in this book, like the exhibits in the Oklahoma History Center, provide lessons learned about the evolution of free enterprise in Oklahoma.

It is clear that resources alone, even with the advantages of markets and location, do not drive the wheels of economic development. Success depends on individual initiative—the ability to deal with challenges and recognize opportunities and the willingness to take a risk whether it is investing time and treasure in an enterprise or developing skills valued in the marketplace.

Individual initiative alone, however, is not enough to create wealth and opportunity that is sustainable. As the stories prove, success depends on our ability to share the benefits of free enterprise. Sometimes that is through partnerships, public service, and philanthropy; sometimes it is through the strength of community action delegated to local, state, tribal, and federal governments. Through the power of partnerships, by giving back to the community, businessmen and businesswomen strengthen the foundations on which our children and grandchildren will look for their opportunities.

Hopefully, they will be willing and able to tackle the challenges, seize the opportunities, and take the risks necessary to conquer new frontiers of free enterprise in Oklahoma.

"I am the Guardian," sculpture on top of the Oklahoma State Capitol
(Photo Marion L. Parker, Yukon)

Index